RETIRED

Hearing Voices

THEATER: Theory/Text/Performance

Enoch Brater, Series Editor
University of Michigan

Hearing Voices

Modern Drama and
the Problem of Subjectivity

John H. Lutterbie

Ann Arbor

THE UNIVERSITY OF MICHIGAN PRESS

To Sara M. Lutterbie
and in memory of
Carlton R. Lutterbie, Jr.

Copyright © by the University of Michigan 1997
All rights reserved
Published in the United States of America by
The University of Michigan Press
Manufactured in the United States of America
⊚ Printed on acid-free paper

2000   1999   1998   1997   4   3   2   1

A CIP catalog record for this book is available from the British Library

Library of Congress Cataloging-in-Publication Data

Lutterbie, John Harry, 1948–
     Hearing voices : modern drama and the problem of subjectivity /
John H. Lutterbie.
        p.   cm. (Theater—Theory/Text/Performance)
     Includes bibliographical references (p.   ) and index.
     ISBN 0-472-10808-5 (cloth)
     1. Drama—20th century—History and criticism.   2. Subjectivity in
literature.   3. Sex role in literature.   4. Identity (Psychology) in
literature.   5. Talk shows.   I. Title.   II. Series.
PN1851.L88   1997
809.2'04—dc21   96-51215
                                                                      CIP

What I want to ask is, Are we able to have an ethics of acts and their pleasures which would be able to take into account the pleasure of the other.

MICHEL FOUCAULT

Everywhere he runs into walls of his palace of mirrors, the floor of which is in any case beginning to crack and break up . . . pretext for an increase in attentiveness, vigilance, mastery. The reason for these quakes must be sought out, these seismic convulsions in the self must be interpreted.

LUCE IRIGARAY

The tracing has already translated the map into an image; it has already transformed the rhizome into roots and radicles. It has organized, stabilized, neutralized the multiplicities according to the axes of significance and subjectification belonging to it.

DELEUZE AND GUATTARI

Acknowledgments

It is impossible adequately to thank the people who influenced the writing of this book. I have had the great fortune to work with, and learn from, some quite exceptional people. Herbert Blau, Sue-Ellen Case, John Burke, Robert Egan, and Francis Hodge have mentored me at different times in my life, opening new perspectives that have immeasurably enriched my thinking. A special thanks to Alan Read, Ellen Donkin, Cass Weller, Lou Charnon-Deutsch, Jerome Tognoli, and Jeanie Forte, who have read and discussed various portions of the book and whose insights created a valuable context in which to think and rethink the ideas presented here. Thanks also to E. Ann Kaplan and my colleagues at the Humanities Institute at Stony Brook, who provided and continue to provide a stimulating and supportive intellectual environment. To my students I owe a special debt for their willingness to engage in a discussion of ideas that, quite frequently, seemed to have little or nothing to do with theater. The discussion of the body in chapter 1 is heavily indebted to the spectacular conjunction of speakers and students involved in the seminar "Performance, Subversive Bodies, and Cultural Difference" (co-taught with Professor Kaplan at the Humanities Institute), which did at times seem more like a lifestyle than a class. I would be remiss if I did not acknowledge the immense support and excellent editorial assistance of LeAnn Fields, Ingrid Erickson, Kristen M. Lare and the University of Michigan Press; and of Herb Blau and Joseph Roach, whose careful reading and generous comments have greatly improved this manuscript.

I would also like to acknowledge those special friendships along the way that have made the going so much easier: Mavourneen Dwyer, Daphne Daniel, John O'Connor, Bill Burford, Anh Pham, Michael Wegner, Scottie and Gordon Wilkison, Janet Snyder, David Smith, Geoff Proehl, and Susan Jonas, as well as my colleagues in the theater arts department at Stony Brook, whose support has been instrumental in the writing of this manuscript. But most of all I wish to give thanks to those who endured most immediately the frustrations of writer's block, the odd hours and temperaments—Simon and Julia, who make life possible, and Sara, whose love and support and insistence that *Hearing Voices* be readable have been unfailing and worthy of every devotion.

Contents

Introduction

Photographs of skeletons from a Nazi concentration camp that emerge from cracks in the streets precipitate the first act of violence in Walter Abish's *How German Is It.* They are shown to Helmuth Hargenau, the architect, and he responds by destroying the photos and throwing Rita Tropf-Ulmwehrt, the photographer, out of the house (Abish 1980, 202–3). His action is simultaneously a recognition of, and a refusal to acknowledge, his complicity in the Holocaust. The specular structure of this resistance is figured in the work of Luce Irigaray: Hargenau, shifting the burden of guilt onto the body of the woman, refuses to let her serve as a mirror in which he may see himself, although he has previously used her to define his subjectivity. His resistance to an inward gaze that might reveal contradictions in the definition of the self necessitates her removal from the scene. Deflecting the implications of her representations of atrocity, Helmuth in effect breaks the mirror to protect a self-image that can no longer sustain itself. He creates a physical and psychological distance that insists upon Rita's alterity and that privileges his own authority.

Irigaray, particularly in her discussion of the masculine and theories of subjectivity, analyzes the configurations of gender and the function of mirroring in defining the male subject, and she muses on the effects of breaking the specular relationship: "But what if the 'object'"—the female object of the gaze—"started to speak?" (1985, 135). What if she shares with him what she sees rather than what he wishes to see? Will he be able to acknowledge the difference, or will he be so "overwhelmed by it as to bar himself out of it and turn it so as to retain at the very least the power to promote his own forms" (135)? For Irigaray there is little question that he will distort the image to insure his "innocence."

This fictional incident and this theoretical moment define the discursive space explored in *Hearing Voices*. At issue is the definition of the subject, which, despite the efforts of contemporary theory to announce its death, refuses to give place either in theory or practice. I do not mean, however, an autonomous subject, the implacable individual idealized in the consumerism of late capitalism, but the intersubject(ive) who depends upon the exchange of reflections for self-imaging. Indeed, this book is about a certain economy, but one that focuses on the landscape of exchange, its constructions and resulting contours, rather than productivity or profitability, although these inevitably inflect the interaction. To extend the economic metaphor, I am exploring the range and quality of the investments we make in difference, and in the desire to maintain our "capital reserves" and our willingness to diversify our range of investments. In this calculus, it is possible to measure the rigidity of the boundaries that separate us and, perhaps, to imagine ways of increasing flexibility.

The assumption underlying the study of this economic geography is that these relations are ultimately and inherently ethical. In an age of postmodern skepticism such an assumption is immediately questioned: on what ground can an ethics be based, given the challenge to metaphysics or any attempt at a totalizing moral system? There is no easy answer. Yet the problem does not go away, unless we are willing to accept physical violence as a resolution to unwanted images of ourselves, to justify atrocity. This position Michel Foucault was unwilling to accept at the end of his life, when he undertook a genealogy of ethics in order to define an aesthetics of the self in relation to others—an ethics that does not depend on a system of universal values.

This book seeks to continue this investigation, not in the form of a genealogy, but through a consideration of subjectivity and the structures by which we preserve our *imago*, the illusory self-image that defines the limits of our bodies and the space of difference between us. I am less interested in the actual limits than the means by which self-images are used to manipulate the space between people, converting difference to distance, defining centers and margins. I am concerned with the ways we fortify the space that separates in order simultaneously to protect our sense of self and to position the "other" so that we maintain the structures of pleasure—which for the moment I loosely define as the positive return on investments in difference. Such relations are not simple binaries, however, but complex constructs in an intricate system of authority and privilege. This system determines not only our position in the relationship but the objects in which, and the intensities with which, we invest. I am not talking about venture capital—the excess we employ to increase wealth—but the structures of our sense of identity, which we continually build and rebuild.

The question of identifications has a long and complicated history in the discourse and definition of the subject. From the myth of Narcissus to identity politics, the concept has been used sometimes separately, sometimes concurrently, to support claims of both individuality and group solidarity. Moreover, it can carry a positive or negative valence, depending on the context in which it is used. This motility of the term, its ability to shift from the singular to the plural, from productive to detrimental, is of interest precisely because identifications are fundamental to our experience of each other and, in large part, are not subject to conscious control. At issue is how the word is deployed and in which contexts it can lead to an understanding of the ideological position of the "speaker," particularly in relation to the person being addressed. And through the definition of location, it seems, we can begin to perceive how the boundaries of difference between the two subjects are constructed—the barriers that are erected or dissolved, that obstruct or facilitate communication. I say "seems" because with identifications it is seldom a question of one or the other. Rather, it frequently appears to be "both . . . and . . ." On the one hand, identifications are seldom, if ever, activated in isolation but appear in bundles of associations, creating complex networks and carrying a multiplicity of charges—positive, negative, and indifferent—in varying intensities. The plurality of valences constellated during an encounter makes ambivalence more likely than simple affiliation or disaffiliation. Therefore, issues of allegiance and difference, of resistance and facilitation, are not easily resolved.

The undecidability of identifications—either their origins or their implications—suggests that the analytics of difference should focus on the structure of an interaction rather than on ontological investigations. This does not mean that a model of subjectivity, its constitution and dynamics, is without value. To the contrary, I believe it is essential to understanding how boundaries and distances are measured. The means by which we shape the limits of our bodies is crucial to determining how we locate ourselves in relation to difference. An investigation of this spatial topography is necessary if a theory of intersubjectivity is to be thought through that will allow us to imagine an aesthetics of the self on which to base an ethics for interacting with others.

The investigation undertaken here begins with the question of the body because ultimately it is the material bodies, of ourselves and others, that are at stake. The move into discourse is too often accompanied by forgetting that the terrain we discuss involves the very real experience of pleasure and pain. But the body, at least in recent discourse, can no longer be taken for granted. Indeed, in some theories the body loses its materiality and becomes a veritable metaphysics of the unrepresentable. I cannot be so sanguine about the disappearance of the material. While I concur that our ability to "know" the body is problematic, I find it impossible to dismiss it, to pretend that it does not affect the materiality of discourse. Indeed, it is a fairly simple exercise to demonstrate that the way in which the body is positioned can determine what we are able to communicate—any stage director worth the name knows how to manipulate actors physically in order to create a desired effect. But as Sue-Ellen Case argues in a recent article on lesbian performance, the current discourse on the body is founded on issues of reception, a privileging of reading over performing (1995a, 8). The purpose of the discussion of the body is not to return to the unmediated, pre-oedipal body of Artaud, of Deleuze and Guattari; it is to insist that bodies are not defined through individual processes but are based on the constructions of similitude and difference that come to be known through interactions with the "other." Our understanding of the body is ultimately an intersubjective construct.

On this ground, however unstable, I examine three modes of constructing and maintaining difference. Chapter 2, a reading of Eric Begosian's *Talk Radio*, explores how Barry Champlain, the talk show host, uses his authority to construct and reconstruct the contours of his self-identity. In the face of an intense existential crisis, Champlain confronts, or rather refuses to confront, a challenge posed by the callers, who do not believe his call to radical change. Envisioning his own death—if only in the dead air of radio silence—Champlain rediscovers his voice, but in speaking creates boundaries of difference that recon-figure his relationship with those that phone him. The shift in his understanding allows him to reimagine himself and allows the reader to perceive the limits of this change. For in refusing the abyss of exis-tential disintegration, the talk show host abandons the community to which he believes himself committed in favor of one he opposes, but to which he is actually and has always been indebted. This reading sug-gests that identifications are the effect of repeated laminations and that the seeming despair when the sense of self collapses is often a passage from one configuration of identity to another. This brief destabilization results, nonetheless, in a piercingly painful crisis, as the intensities of investment are wrested from one "object" and fixed on another. This movement, I argue, far from implying a free fall, is actually a recogni-tion that we are always standing on solid ground, and that the change is one of affiliations, the ways in which we construct the boundaries of difference between the self and others.

The issue of affiliation as an effect of gender construction is explored in the third chapter. Sam Shepard's *A Lie of the Mind* has received serious attention from a number of feminists who see in this work the outlines of profeminist discourse. Utilizing different interpre-tations of the way space is used in the scenic design articulated by the playwright and Shepard's recorded thoughts about feminism, these critics attempt to recuperate the text, claiming to see within its horizons an empowering of women that promises at its furthest reaches the utopian possibility of equality between the sexes. While acknowledg-ing the value of such images in defining a discourse in which the dis-appearance of sexual bias can be imagined, I pose a different reading. Instead of a horizon of possibility, I perceive a reinscription of differ-ence that has more in common with the male separatism of Robert Bly's mythopoetic movement than a kinship with feminist programs of change. Given Bly's claim that he is responding to the demands of fem-inism for increased male sensitivity to issues of gender, his appropria-tion of "feminine" caring as a "masculine" attribute is intriguing. Far from opening spaces of possible equality, Bly and Shepard conceal in narratives of change structures that resist giving agency to women.

Through Jean Genet's *The Balcony* I explore the use of narrative to perpetuate discourses of difference. Here the stories of interest are not those that move the action of the play; rather, they are those through which the characters construct fantasies that provide them with sexual release. The role of pleasure in the constitution of the subject implies that the value of the narrative lies in the structures of fantasy that promise more than an escape from the mundane. Choosing to enact a bishop, judge, general, or beggar in order to play out a scenario of libidinal release indicates an investment in the reality of these social functions, because without their place in the culture they would not be available for use in the studios of the Balcony. The appropriation of the garments of public office for the satisfaction of desire bespeaks a dependence on the existing political order. Indeed, I contend that there is an inherent conservatism in the definition of subjectivity because it is defined, in the last instance, by our interpellation into the structures of the society in which we live.

The tentative conclusions reached through the discussions of talking, appropriation, and fantasy serve as a basis for defining a theory of the subject. Employing the phantasmaphysics of Deleuze and Guattari, I argue for a material subjectivity constituted through assemblages that provide sequences that, in turn, provide a release of energy, however incomplete, on "appropriate" objects of desire. Utilizing Freud's theory of the instincts in conjunction with concepts derived from neurophysiology, I read Samuel Beckett's *Not I* as a discourse on the necessity of difference and its devastating effects when used to marginalize people who fail to conform to culturally accepted standards.

The final chapter asks that we look at our own complicity in the definition of differences and the effects those definitions have on the ability of others to express themselves as subjects. The tendency to conserve relations of difference in order to perpetuate narratives of pleasure appears to be a major obstacle to imagining a more equal economy of intersubjective relations. It is here that Michel Foucault's aesthetics of subjectivity comes into play. He asks whether or not it is possible to conceive of a subjectivity that takes into account the well-being of the "other." The issue is ultimately ethical, but with very material consequences. If subjectivity is based, as I contend, on avenues of expression that historically provide pleasure, then is it possible to construct differently our relationship with those conceived of as different, so that they too can experience pleasure in our interactions with them? There is little room for optimism. Nevertheless, it remains one of the central issues in a postmodern world where ethics appear bankrupt and the pursuit of individual wealth—regardless of the cost to the well-being of others—is a dominant motivating force. It appears to me that if change is possible, it must be allowed to happen. When relations of power are affected, when resistance is encountered, we must explore alternatives to structures of difference that result in a politics of marginalization. This, in turn, necessitates an opening of spaces—real and discursive—in which others can experience themselves as subjects. It means a willingness to retreat; to locate new forms of pleasure that do not require a repetition of the same; to surrender identifications and, therefore, live a more fluid, destabilized subjectivity. Herein lies the pessimism. But we may find that more flexible boundaries of difference, an impulse to inclusion rather than exclusion, provides pleasures of its own.

A politics of retreat is possible only if those in authority who resist exercising their privilege step back and wait. In contemporary theoretical discourse, the contested lines of authority are identified literally and metaphorically with the structurings of patriarchy. The tendency to vilify white, heterosexual men continues as a common discursive practice despite the arguments of men who resist being placed in reductive categories that deny a multiplicity of subjectivities, and the reluctant recognition that relations of power tend to reproduce themselves regardless of who is in authority. Nevertheless, men must bear responsibility for perpetrating reprehensible and violent acts of oppression in the exercise of macro- and micropolitical power. This explains, in part, my decision to use plays authored by men as the primary objects of analysis. It is most certainly not because women have nothing to say about subjectivity—in plays or in theory. Rather, I believe that it is preferable to understand the strategies by which differences are inscribed and maintained through texts written by those who traditionally, and in many cases presently, exercise authority.

It will be argued that Jean Genet, a self-proclaimed homosexual, hardly fits in this category, and I would not disagree. However, it is not specifically because of his homosexuality that Genet should be either included or excluded. The value of Genet's perspective is the intensity with which he sought to construct his identity outside of the law—both social and heterosexual. His determination to embrace abjection and eroticism as the basis for a radical alterity provides him with a unique vantage point from which to examine the structuring of society and the circulations of intensities—sexual and authoritarian—that perpetuate systems of difference and objectification.

Also open to question is the decision to privilege the "minor"

genre of the drama as an object of study. Plays, more than other forms
of literature, are principally explorations of behavior, of how people
act—the choices they make, their motivations and consequences. This
is, in part, because they are necessarily written in the first-person singular, present indicative. They happen "now" and are not available to
the descriptive rationalizations of memory. At the center of every play
is the human subject and how s/he lives his/her life is in question.
Even a text as distilled as Samuel Beckett's *Breath*—with its screams "in
vagitus" amid the detritus of a compulsive consumerism—happens
now and reflects, however abstractly, on the choices we make and the
means by which we cushion ourselves from the experiences of birth
and death, of pain. That is the nature of the beast, because plays are
written for live actors—even if their only function is to be recorded
screaming into a microphone. The body in motion is always the measure, regardless of how political, transcendent, abstract, or absurd.

The forms of behavior represented in plays needs a greater degree
of precision because the writing is considerably more compressed and
is most frequently dialogic. Even when there is a narrator who
describes the ground on which the character stands, s/he is located in
an interactive frame that foregrounds the conflicts engaged in determining how to act. Each utterance acknowledges the distance between
the performer and the context in which it takes place, what Keir Elam
calls the "possible world" of the play—a construct that sustains enough
congruences between the experience of the spectators and those of the
characters to make the world of the play acceptably "real" (Elam 1980,
100).

Unlike the novel, however, which also constructs possible worlds,
the play is subject to the pressures of the temporal. Within the real time
of speech the performance needs to produce an image, a signification,
that audience members can comprehend within the context of the play
and their own experience, link with events in a fictional past, and project
on an equally fictional future. There is little time for reflection. A key to
the craft of playwriting is the ability to imagine and condense into language the complexities of human behavior. Nothing will take an audience member out of a play more quickly than actions that do not make
sense within the frame of the text. Ionesco's *Bald Soprano* succeeds in
exploring the absurdity of human communication precisely because
there is no congruity between the words and the activities of the characters—a disjunction that, ironically, makes his critique of behavior

understandable. Underlying the rhetoric of the narrative in the drama is the ability to believe the characters. If Harold Pinter is to be believed, there is nothing more distressing for a playwright than to get a character "wrong," to distort the behavioral logic of a character's trajectory.

There is another level of scrutiny to which plays are exacted that other literary genres are not: performance. Plays are written to be embodied by actors, and the force of a character is dependent upon the performer's ability to reconcile the action required in the "world" of the play with the actor's life experience. When first performed, plays are frequently rewritten because of inconsistencies in the playwright's text and the actor's ability to justify in performance the choices made by a character. The actor's resistance to a particular line or choice is seldom casual, but is symptomatic of a breakdown in the complex system of reflections founded on what the actor considers possible. The point I wish to make is that seldom is a play the singular vision of the playwright; it has undergone a filtering process involving actors, directors, and dramaturgs, who seek an adequate definition of the specific relationship that must exist between the text and the dominant paradigms of behavior of the culture in which the play is written. The theater, therefore, is a crucible in which the mettle of a play is tested on and in the bodies of the performers, a re-visioning of the text to reflect more adequately the institutions and lines of authority that limit the forms of subjectivity available to characters and playwrights.

To engage the subjectivities and intersubjectivities that shape the form and delimit the range of contents available in a play is to ponder the patterns of behavior and the attitudes toward those behaviors prevalent in cultural forms—forms that *determine* the limitations imposed on the playwright's ability to imagine relations between people. In reading those relationships it is possible to unearth the strategies through which boundaries of difference are defined and enforced, to better understand the lines of authority and repression that create a need for an aesthetics of subjectivity and an ethics that allows for intersubjective interactions that resist the silencing of others.

Chapter 1

Bodies

A book about subjectivity and an ethics of intersubjectivity should begin with a discussion of the body, especially in the age of AIDS, of cyborgs and virtual realities, when the integrity of the body is put into question. At stake, ultimately, are boundaries and limits: What can we know of the body? At what point does discourse impose limits on what is knowable about the body? To what extent does the material body determine our ability to engage in discourse? Such questions are not easily answered, nor are they likely to be resolved in the near future. These indeterminacies do not, of course, free us from engaging in these debates, nor is it acceptable merely to position ourselves on one side or the other, and claim that the opposition is irrelevant—a strategy all too often employed. To deny the materiality of the body is as absurd as to claim that knowledge can be articulated outside of discourse. The truth of both positions indicates that any theory of the body must always be considered provisional. Any discussion of the body depends on where you locate yourself—like physical theories of light: from one perspective light appears to be made of particles, from another it consists of waves.

From the modernist perspective, the body is an object that can never be adequately contained by language. The body always exceeds the parameters of any one discourse, or combination of discourses. It is Artaud's dream, as read by Herbert Blau, to locate "a body that is only body"; he "wants the body there in its delirium, sonorous flesh streaming, not as representing but in the absence of (its) representation" (Blau 1992, 105). The impossibility of locating the ontological, not to say essential, body free from the "contaminations" of discourse leads post-modern theorists to question the very existence of the material body. In postmodernism as defined by Kroker and Cook, the body is not a bio-logical organism, but an assemblage, articulated and existing as an entity only in the discourse, and the context, in which it is conceptual-ized.

> The body is a power grid, tattooed with all the signs of cultural excess on its surface, encoded from within by the language of desire, broken into at will by the ideological interpellation of the subject, and, all the while, held together as a fictive concrete unity by the illusion of *misrecognition*. (1988, 26)

And yet even their eloquent evocation of an assembled body cannot totally escape the ontological body. Implicit in Kroker and Cook is a "grid" that can be "tattooed," "encoded," and "broken into"; that has a "within" and, therefore, an outside. It is the ineluctable return of the body's materiality that Blau calls the "pull of the organism" (1992, 120), and that leads him to claim,

> I am in my body the way that is simply inescapable, not to be deferred or lost as on the freeway in the metonymic appearances of a referential chain, nor reconstituted in the eternity of ideology as a linguistic subject, though I am that, too, to all appearances, which keep us tautologically in the double bind. (121)

It is the same double bind that Judith Butler confronts in arguing for the subversive potential of the performative in the constitution of gender categories.

Performance and Performativity

Butler, in *Bodies That Matter*, engages the discursive formations of West-ern thought both classical and contemporary, from Aristotle to Fou-cault, from Lacan to Irigaray. Her strategy is to read key texts rigor-ously, paying careful attention to the tropes and the contradictions elided in the formulation of the arguments. For instance, in a close reading of Lacan's conceptualization of the phallus, Butler argues persuasively for a lesbian phallus, deterritorializing Lacan's symbol of male power. This subversive act releases a potential for agency traditionally reserved for representatives of patriarchal domination, demonstrating that the position of the subject can be occupied by lesbians, indeed by populations representing a multiplicity of genders. Butler, by showing the false pretext on which homosexual women have been marginalized through discourse, further empowers lesbians to engage in performative acts that enact their existence in a culture that pathologizes the very possibility of their being.

However, even as she argues for the power of discourse to define the reality of the body as the performance of gender inscriptions, Butler is forced to acknowledge the existence of a nondiscursive force that can only be the body.

> Always already caught up in the signifying chain by which sexual difference is negotiated, the anatomical is never given outside its terms, and yet it is also that which exceeds and compels that signifying chain, that reiteration of difference, an insistent and inexhaustible demand. (1993, 90)

This persistent return of the anatomical as a force with which to be reckoned causes Blau to affirm the "surpassing body," "that impertinent presence which constitutes the expressiveness of codes or the apparent life-force or vitality of signs" (1992, 120).

This energetics of the body defines excess for the modernist and the grid of intensity for the postmodernist. Although for the former this "vitality" makes the question of subjectivity impossible to resolve and for the latter it identifies a basis for constructing a theory of subjectivity, the persistance of this "life-force" necessitates its consideration. And nowhere is this necessity more evident than in the tendency to conflate performance and performativity.

Performativity, at least as conceived by J. L. Austin, is a discursive operation that brings states of being into existence through speech acts. "I hereby name thee . . ."—which, if a felicitous act, attaches a name to an object. For Austin, a performative happens only once, because the state, having been brought into being, can only be reinscribed through repetitions that cannot alter the situation. For instance, the first time we embraced the letter "J" as a nickname for my daughter Julia, a new state came into existence. Further uses of the moniker merely reinforce the decision to address her by using her first initial—nothing is changed. The act of naming, the performative, can only happen once. To further isolate a speech act from other behaviors and acts, Austin distinguishes between intention, which he perceives as unknowable and unimportant provided the utterance is felicitous, and the effect of the performative, which is equally insignificant provided the context in which the act occurs will support the felicity of the signification. Specifying the speech act allows Austin to sidestep issues of performance and, for all practical purposes, reception, while usefully identifying how particular grammatical constructions operate. To return to the example of my daughter, for Austin, why we used the letter "J" to refer to her is unimportant, as is anyone's distaste for the decision. What is significant is that there is sufficient consensus for the nickname to stick, because then the act has felicity and my daughter is stuck, at least for a time, being called "J."

When Judith Butler takes up the concept in both *Gender Trouble* and *Bodies That Matter*, the performative is extended beyond linguistic acts to include bodily acts. Appearing in drag, for instance, becomes a performative that subverts traditional gendered roles by bringing into being a state that disturbs and multiplies the gender possibilities defined by the traditional heterosexual matrix. The power of drag, however, lies in deferring the naming of the act. Its force lies precisely in its resistance to being named, its infelicity. The question is: Once the performative occurs, once the drag performance is acknowledged, named, does the act cease to subvert? Signification alters experience by limiting the range of meanings to culturally prescribed boundaries— the performance becomes performative. What is lost when the semiotic screen comes to dominate the performing body? This may, in part, be the reason why in *Bodies That Matter* she confronts the issue of language, bodies, and materiality, concluding that "always already implicated in each other, always already exceeding one another, language and materiality are never fully identical nor fully different" (Butler 1993, 69). Nevertheless, Butler resists discussing what if any influence the material might exert in the definition of subjectivity.

> The body in the mirror does not represent a body that is, as it were, before the mirror: the mirror, even as it is instigated by that unrep-

> resentable body "before" the mirror, produces that body as its
> delirious effect—a delirium, by the way, which we are compelled
> to live. (Butler 1993, 91)

But how are we to understand this delirium? Is it merely another way of figuring *jouissance,* of (not) coping with the concept of excess?

In focusing on what can be said rather than the act of saying, Butler elides the body by denying its specificity, and risks, once again, rendering it invisible. The desire to maintain a material presence has encouraged some lesbians to embrace a "situated" essentialism. "De Lauretis counters the charge of essentialism by distinguishing a 'nominal essence' in contrast to a 'real' one, that would, within a feminist project, proffer an 'embodied, situated knowledge,' as mutable and historically contextualized" (Case 1995a, 3). The need to reconfigure essentialism underlines the tension between those who embrace the performativity of gender and those who insist the lesbian body is more than an effect of discourse. There is, within this debate, an insistence on the need to distinguish between performing and performativity, between the body that acts and the body that is enacted. To insist on an absolute distinction may be folly; but to deny the difference seems equally dangerous.

If performativity is bringing into existence a state of being through an act, whether linguistic or a subversion of gender, performance is precisely the act: the doing that enacts the signification. Joseph Roach, in a discussion of headshots used by actors and models to secure work, figures the difference this way.

> The photographic image, created in a performative moment, records the effects of many rehearsals, retakes, and preparations. The headshot thus records a long-running performance, the creation of a fictive persona, cleansed of superfluities, the special residue that many call a life. (Roach 1995, 153)

This is not to say, as Roach well understands, that the body being photographed is not "a long-running performance, the creation of a fictive persona," but rather that the performative is a purification, a reduction of what Roland Barthes calls the "grain of the voice" to a surface that intones an image, an image that is stripped of performance even as it is a record of it.

The problem facing theorists of performance is the difficulty in finding a language adequate to the discussion of this remainder. The dependence on metaphor in efforts to define the discourse—grain of the voice, *jouissance,* aesthetics of excess, the plague—allows critics to assert that such theories are ultimately based in metaphysics and, having no foundation in material reality, are mere flights of fantasy lacking in rigor. I will argue that far from (re)defining a metaphysics, the "sticky organicity" of this remainder is the very stuff of materiality and that its effects not only instigate but shape, in very concrete ways, the representable body and its attendant delirium.

Performance and Reception

The negation of the performing body in the name of performativity has its antecedents in reception theory, whether in textual criticism or film and media studies. With the much heralded death of the author, focus in the study of printed texts shifted away from interpretations based in structural analysis that sought to discern the mark of the person who wrote it. Interest in the text as an object of study was superseded by attention to the ways in which the text is constructed as a reflection of the particular historical context and ideological practices of the reader. The analysis of cinema, with its particular emphasis on the theory of the "gaze," approaches issues of textuality in similar ways, the most significant differences being that shifting iconographic images produced by the play of light on the screen replace the clustering of linguistic images on the printed page. In either form, the presence of the "performer" (author/actor/director) is not only unnecessary, but often a distraction. Coincident with these developments in critical analysis was a proliferation of interest in the screen, as postmodern theories sought to account for the growing pervasiveness of surfaces in mediated experiences. The disruptions caused by this paradigmatic shift from linguistic description to iconographic representation brought new attention to the representations of the body—but a body that loses its three-dimensionality in the process of mediation. It is the displacement of the performing body in the shift to what is discursively significant on the screen that may explain the interest in the performative. However, reception theorists are discovering that what is omitted in discussions of representation is precisely what they need to account for in defining the act of interpretation: the performing body. The recognition that interpretation is a performance necessitates, once again, a considera- tion of the performing body, and how that body shapes the process of reception.

One aspect of this "shaping" is explored by N. Katherine Hayles, who investigates the discourse surrounding computer technologies and, therefore, the question of screens from the perspective of interac- tivity. In so doing she unveils the Cartesian idealism behind visions of virtual reality. She locates in the discussions on virtuality a desire to actualize the mind-body split of the Western enlightenment, that is, the literal negation of the body. Whether, as in recent science fiction, it is separating the body by downloading the human psyche into the microchips of cyberspace or of computer implants that alter personality and cognitive structures, Hayles finds a pervasive belief that we can either do without the body or that the mind can be sufficiently enhanced to exert absolute control over the biological organism. Turn- ing to "real" science, she cites the work of Hans Moravec, head of the Carnegie-Mellon Mobile Robot Laboratory, who believes, one day, humans will be able to escape the dread of death through immortality in computer technology.

> Humans need not despair, however, because they can have their consciousness downloaded into a computer. In the fantastic sce- nario in which he imagines this operation, Moravec has a robot surgeon cut away a human brain in a kind of cranial liposuction until all the information the brain contained is inside the computer and the skull is empty of brain tissue. (Hayles 1994, 2)

Hayles argues that even if it proves possible to replicate processes of thought, the subjectivity "living" in cyperspace will bear little resem- blance to the embodied subject. She echoes computer artist Catherine Richards, whose work in creating virtual environments "comes not only from her insistence on materiality but also from her implicit assumption that body and mind interact and that any reconfiguration of the body must necessarily affect how subjectivity is constituted" (Hayles 1994, 27). Hayles holds not only that the neural connectors are necessary for the transmission of perceptual data to the brain, but that the body is a memory system and that perceptual experiences are inscribed on the musculature and organs of the body. Furthermore, this "writing" is central to the experience of subjectivity. Far from a Luddite, however, Hayles envisions the "posthuman," which involves not the elimination of the body, but the

> realizations that await us when the dialectic between presence/absence is integrated with the dialectic of pattern/randomness. Put another way, the posthuman represents the construction of the body as part of an integrated information/material circuit that includes human and non-human components, silicon chips as well as organic tissue, bits of information as well as bits of flesh and bone. (Hayles 1994, 17)

What remains inescapable is the physical body, regardless of how cyborgian and regardless of prosthetics. The body is not the equivalent of electrical circuitry that processes information because the corporeal is actively engaged in the gathering and processing of data and the production of meaning.

The place of the body in reception is also explored by Peggy Phelan, who in *Unmarked: The Politics of Performance* seeks to define the "ontology" of performance by mapping the effects of loss on the terrain of the body. Haunted by the inevitable disappearance of performance and therefore the representable body, Phelan seeks to track the effects/affects of performance and the possible range of meanings attributable to the temporal and the absent. She is specifically interested in gender and the semiotic negation of the woman's body in dominant discourses. The angst of losing the desired object may explain her preference for photographs or the installations of performers like Angelica Festa, whose work investigates the seeming suspension of time, repetition and stillness. In the continuity of Festa's images—which both resist and hold out the promise of representation—Phelan locates the possibility of a communication between the "present" bodies of the performer and spectator.

> The spectator's inability to meet the eye *defines* the other's body as lost; the pain of this loss is underlined by the corollary recognition that the represented body is so manifestly and painfully there, for both Festa and the spectator. Festa cannot see her body because her eyes are taped shut; the spectator cannot see Festa and must gaze

instead at the wrapped shell of a lost eyeless body. (Phelan 1993, 156)

What Phelan seeks in the event is the trace of the "unmarked," the remainder that exceeds representation, locating in the "unnamable" of performance the site where understanding is possible. But it is an imprecise communication, based on a necessary misrecognition, whose meaning is ultimately determined by the act of reception.

It is Phelan who describes the event, who ascribes intentions and interprets. Festa remains silent, a "wrapped shell." Perhaps this is because the performing body can be reconstituted only in the space between its disappearance and the memory of it, regardless of who is talking, the performer or the spectator. Nevertheless, the silence of the performer—perhaps Festa prefers not to talk about her work—places less emphasis on the acts of the performer's body, and more on the performance of reception, on the attribution of meaning by the spectator. Phelan is eloquent about what she sees in Festa's work, articulating powerful interpretations evoked through empathy with the performer's pain and through images constelled in the space between the performative body and the tangible—Phelan *feels* a connection—but unrepresentable performance.

Ironically, here is precisely where Phelan elides her own performing body and the effects of the physical on her perception of the performance. Pervasive throughout *Unmarked* is the privileging of seeing. While this is not an uncommon trope, given the fetishization of the female body and the emphasis on the scopic drive in contemporary theory, equally significant is her own experience when an "infection in my left eye passed the blood-brain barrier" (Phelan 1995, 202). The fear of losing vision, of not seeing (and not being seen—"a lost eyeless body"), not as a metaphor but a physical reality outside of discourse, allows for the creation of an empathetic connection with the sightless Festa, making the body's experience a factor in Phelan's perception of the performance and her decision to privilege this event over others. As with Hayles, the corporeal—as well as the psychic—inscriptions of experience effect the cognitive process, despite our inability to read specifically the marks of those influences.

If there is difficulty in reading the force of the corporeal in our own cognitive processes, how much more difficult it must be to gauge this

pressure in the actions of others. Yet this is precisely the challenge presented by performing bodies: the necessity of engaging what Phelan
calls the "unmarked."

> The unmarked is not spatial; nor is it temporal; it is not metaphor-
> ical; nor is it literal. It is a configuration of subjectivity which
> exceeds, even while informing, both the gaze and language. In the
> riots of sound language produces, the unmarked can be heard as
> silence. In the plenitude of pleasure produced by photographic
> vision, the unmarked can be seen as a negative. In the analysis of
> the means of production, the unmarked signals the un(re)produc-
> tive. (1993, 27)

Phelan locates these signals in the space of disappearance, understanding them to be intensities that are discernable in the distance between
the poles of the physical and the psyche. They are discernable but not
subject to representation in discourse because their silence defines
them as unmarkable. "Performance uses the performer's body to pose
a question about the inability to secure the relation between subjectivity and the body *per se*" (1993, 151). The tension created by the impossibility of reconciling "who I am" with "what I am" makes the spectator
aware of potentials, however unrealized or unrealizable, that signal the
difference between the experience of self and the limitations on representation imposed by cultural discourses.

The difficulty Phelan encounters is how to give "voice" to these
intensities. Her resolution is a privileging of psychoanalytic discourse,
specifically Freud's concept of the symptom. The purpose of performance (art) in this context is the staging of the symptom, thereby allowing the "unmarked" to have a hearing.

> The symptom's meaning emerges in relation to the psychoanalytic
> dialogue: it is not so much that the dialogue produces the symp-
> tom's meaning, but rather the dialogue creates a stage upon which
> the symptom's meaning can be amplified. This amplification dis-
> torts the sound the symptom makes—but it does provide a hear-
> ing. (Phelan 1993, 168)

The question is, as always, what is heard and who is hearing? The psychoanalytic discourse is extremely powerful and contextualizes any dia-

logue in a relatively precise framework. To what extent is it possible to determine the degree of distortion? And given the silence in which the voice of disappearance is heard, can we be sure a dialogue is happening? The silence of Festa in the account of her work and the articulate interpretation of that work by Phelan raises the question of whether a dialogue occurs—or are we engaged in a mirror game in which Phelan sees not Festa's disappearance, but the enunciation of her own discursive positions? I do not wish to underestimate the value of the experience in defining a feminist politics; and if that is what the performance achieved, if only for Phelan, it is certainly noteworthy. Nor is it possible, in reading the account, to escape, even through a vicarious reconstruction, the implicit power of the installation. But in privileging the unmarked there is a danger of returning to a metaphysics of presence with its promise of unmediated communication and the illusion of a dialogue.

These concerns do not minimize the significance of Phelan's discussion of the necessary relationship between the corporeal and the cognitive in both the receiver and the performer. Indeed, it is precisely the unmarked that underlies the perceptual interface between body and technology in the work of Hayles and that lies at the heart of Blau's theories of performance. "I mean now something 'beyond' or 'prior to' structure *in* the structure, as if between word and breath, the knowledge that can't be discredited because it's there, you know it's there, in and out of performance" (Blau 1982b, 197). It is the unmarked that defines the qualitative difference between the live performer and the screened image.

I do not wish to mythologize live performance, but few would deny that there is a significant difference between electronically mediated images and the "presence" of the actor. And while the difference is difficult to measure, it is nonetheless tangible, "something-more-and-other-than-what-was-done, and yet *that* presence, the thing itself, tactile, palpable, inarguably *there*" (Blau 1982a, 37). The live body defines an experience that extends beyond the performative, beyond the desire to reduce theater to a semiotic screen. While this remainder, excess, unmarked defines a persistent difference between the performative and performance, it is clearly insufficient as a definition of performance or of the body. What is lacking is that which makes the performative part of performance: consciousness itself. "What is universal in performance is the consciousness of performance" (Blau 1987, 171). When Blau makes this statement, he is not alluding to a Cartesian intellect somehow separable from the organicity of the doubtable body, but of an embodied intellect. "But that's to understand that the intellect is also carnal, and that cerebral (etymologically) has genital roots" (Blau 1982a, 34–35). "The thing we're talking about—in theatre and reading, *the thought of performance*—is carnal, skin-close, intestinal, pulsed, not superimposed upon a text" (Blau 1982a, 33).

It is here that, for me, Phelan's binary of the physical and psychic—which she must maintain in defining the unmarked—falls short. The unmarked is perceived as an energetics that precedes (she is defining an ontology of performance) or is at least outside of discourse, as if the affects of the body somehow escape the pressures of consciousness. Certainly the body precedes consciousness, but once the act of differentiation occurs—which is not the imposition of a foreign process but an act of the body—and choices begin to be made between ideological practices, it becomes increasingly difficult to maintain that priority. As I shall argue, resistances in the mind create affects in the body, as much as the body shapes choices. I see my son watching himself in the mirror, determining the "coolest" way to poise the ends of his sunglass frames in his mouth. It is not simply an intellectual process about which looks best, but a complex interaction of desire, image, organic structure, ideological pressures that will determine the stylistics of his body, of his thought, of his interactions—inescapably physical *and* intellectual—with others. In other words, what is perceived as unmarked, which is unmarked, is still affected in its form and expression by the ways in which we have been marked. Memory, for instance, is not simply the cathecting of specific neural paths that bring back to mind the traces of a past event; but an interplay of desire, of muscular tensions, of the responsiveness of specific organs and of intellectual processes.

It is this carnal intellect that decides upon the locution that brings into being the performative utterance. It is the substantiation of the performative that defines the structures of corporeality in the performance of gender, of race, of class. What needs to be argued, and this is a focus of this book, are the processes—physical, psychic, and intellectual—that determine the performing body, its performances and performatives. The danger in such a discussion is that of the totalizing gesture, of acting as if the body were all bodies. And while I believe there are certain processes universal to all conscious beings, there is the humbling need to realize the vast differences between individual bodies.

Modeling Sexual Difference

Elizabeth Grosz confronts the question of difference in *Volatile Bodies: Toward a Corporeal Feminism.* The main part of the work is an examination of the dominant (male) theories of the body and subjectivity, demonstrating the limitations of the current theoretical models in explaining sexual difference. She uses the trope of a Möbius strip—a strip of material looped with a single twist in it so that what is the inside at one point becomes the outside at another—to divide major approaches to the body. This useful image allows her to differentiate those theories that approach sexual difference from the inside out, such as the psychoanalytic, and those that approach it from the outside in, such as theories that emphasize social constraints in the determination of gender. She contends that both are inadequate because although they claim to provide structures for understanding sexual difference, their constructs tend to universalize subjectivity, using male experience as paradigmatic for all people. Through the privileging of the masculine, the experiences of women are either cast in a negative light, as in concepts of lack, or assumed to be identical with men. Grosz, in rejecting the reductiveness of these models, offers an alternative paradigm: bodily fluids.

The value of using bodily fluids as a basis for defining sexual differences is twofold. First, it has a material base. There are distinct differences, as well as similarities, in the fluids of men's and women's bodies, particularly those associated with sexual specificity: semen, vaginal lubrications, menstrual flows. Second, there are cultural discourses about bodily fluids—she pays particular attention to constructions of the clean and the dirty—that are useful in understanding the social inscriptions of gender and the articulation of sexual hierarchies in specific cultures. The immediate value of her model is that it is not based on a negation. Women and men are understood to be equal but different, and access to agency and subjectivity is perceived as culturally and not sexually determined. This insistence on distinct sexes also avoids the tendency to conflate the very different experiences of women and men in the act of theorization.

Grosz does not make inflated claims for her model, recognizing instead the limitations of all models.

A model is a heuristic device which facilitates a certain understanding, highlighting certain features while diminishing the significance of others; it is a selective rewriting of a situation whose
complexity entails the possibility of other, alternative models,
models which highlight different features, presenting different
emphases. (1994, 209)

Moreover, she acknowledges that her setting forth of bodily fluids as a
basis for a theory of sexual difference is in its initial stages of articulation. Grosz does not assert that her new paradigm has been fully conceptualized. That being said, there are certain tendencies in her theory
that replicate some of the problems she locates in the dominant theoretical positions she critiques; these problems argue for a more complex
model of sexual difference than her formulation will allow.

Writing about sexual difference implies an authorial position that is
going to be complicated by the personal experience of being sexual and
gendered. Inherent in this truth is the fact that there are limits to the
knowledge we can have about those across the sex and gender divide.

The problematic of sexual difference entails a certain failure of
knowledge to bridge the gap, the interval, between the sexes.
There remains something ungraspable, something outside, unpredictable, and uncontainable, about the other sex for each sex.
(Grosz 1994, 208)

In the articulation of this interval between sexes, Grosz maintains the
polarity of male and female. This strategy has the unfortunate effect of
reinscribing the heterosexual matrix as a "natural" relationship and
invoking the structures of sexual oppression implicit in that discourse.
Furthermore, by acknowledging an interval of unknowability in the
male/female binary, she exacerbates an already oppositional relationship between the sexes.

This may be intentional given her avowedly feminist stance; but it
results in the same kind of reductionist imaging of men Grosz decries
in men's representations of women.

It may help explain the alienness of men's capacity to reify bodily
organs, to be interested in organs rather than the subjects to whom
they belong, to seek sexuality without intimacy, to strive for

anonymity amid promiscuity, to detach themselves from sexual engagement in order to establish voyeuristic distance, to enjoy witnessing and enacting violence and associate it with sexual pleasure, to enjoy the idea or actuality of sex with children, as an act of conscious cruelty, to use their sexual organs as weapons (and indeed to produce weapons modeled on the image of the sexual organs). (Grosz 1994, 200)

Granted she is talking about "men's *capacity*"; and it would be unfair to attribute to Grosz the claim that this is what men *are*. But there is no statement to suggest men have other capacities as well, nor is there any sense that these capacities could be attributable to women. I am not insisting that Grosz needs to be fair. Given the statistics and bodily experiences of women, there is certainly a general validity to her charge. The difficulty with such rhetorical strategies is that they fortify binary relations, concretizing distances between subjects, changing intervals into abysses. I believe there are more constructive ways of dealing with the interval that separates men from women.

Perhaps more important, however, the definition of a particular axis privileges the poles and other divisions are rendered less significant if not invisible. For instance, in her discussion of transsexuals, Grosz reduces the experience of being transsexual to a metaphor for the impossibility of bridging male and female experiences. "At best the transsexual can live out his fantasy of femininity—a fantasy that in itself is usually disappointed with the rather crude transformations effected by surgical and chemical intervention. The transsexual may look like a woman but can never feel like or be a woman" (Grosz 1994, 207). Given her insistence on the incommensurability of the sexes, how she can say with certainty what a transsexual may or may not feel or experience is questionable—as is the implication that all transsexuals are men trying to become women. More to the point, the transsexual becomes in this argument a caesura, an untransgressable break, in the line that connects male and female. The androgyne, the illusory center point in the continuum from one sex to the other, is replaced by the transsexual who marks the impossibility of such a trajectory. However, by deploying the transsexual in this way, Grosz denies the possibility of a continuum while she implies that all sexualities are situated along this axis. There is no space outside of the male/female dichotomy to locate alternative sexualities.

The one male body has become two bodies—male and female.
While this division is certainly an advance over dominant patriarchal
systems of thought, it is inadequate to a discussion of sexual difference.
It needs to be acknowledged that there is a multiplicity of sexualities
and that the experiences of those bodies mark differences that are not
compatible with a binary construct. As homosexuals and lesbians
insist, it is inappropriate to assume that all men and women experience
in the same way. Similarly, transsexuals, bisexuals, and intersexuals
(hermaphrodites) cannot be positioned neatly along a continuum
defined by a binary. A theory of sexuality needs a multidimensional
model that will allow for similarities of experience as well as differences, that will resist totalizing gestures and acknowledge "something
ungraspable, something outside, unpredictable, and uncontainable."

There is, of course, a limit to which any theoretical model can
accommodate individualities. Any theory of the body must face the
inescapable tendency to generalize, negating the marks of difference.
This "necessity" is exacerbated by the limits of language and the need
to accommodate similarities as well as differences. And nowhere is this
more evident than in the words *men* and *women*. These terms simultaneously mark a radical separation and the negation of a multitude of
differences. So problematic are these words that it is almost a liability to
use them, and yet not to use them, to qualify their meaning, is to make
the act of theorizing unacceptably cumbersome. To articulate, specifically, *which* men are being signified is both necessary and impossible,
since it requires defining not only sexuality, but race, class, ethnic background, and so forth. The options are few. Among the most unattrac-
tive are either the creation of a plethora of neologisms and acronyms
that will further obfuscate already difficult projects, or risk the inaccuracies of the totalizing gesture.

The definition of an authorial position can ameliorate the negative
potentials implicit in the "universal" body by keeping before the reader
the particularity that underlies the discourse. To identify myself as a
white, middle-class, heterosexual man does not protect my writing
from the prejudices my position exerts on the theory I write, but it can
encourage the readers to use their own specificity as a mark against
which to evaluate my positions while simultaneously reminding the
readers that their specificity incurs as many liabilities as my own. This
tension can destabilize in a productive way by continually underlining

the uncertainties and limitations in any discourse on the body. Furthermore, it recognizes that there are only bodies and not "the" body.

> *The* body stands still, like a statue, or lies in repose, like a corpse. As a metaphysical abstraction or a bracketed phenomenon, its essence transcends in action, its color, its features, its history, its desire, its transactions, and its pain. A plenitude of bodies, by contrast, suggests multiple possibilities of movement, interaction, combination, circulation, and exchange. Just to begin to make the list of the diversity and the reciprocity of bodies is to question the totality of the body. (Roach 1995, 150)

The downside of an insistence on particularity is the immanent threat of relativity: all bodies are so different it is impossible to make any reasonable claims about them. To differentiate is impossible without some underlying foundation of similarity. The unresolvable problem is how to identify the range of similarities. Male homosexuals are certainly men, for instance, but to assume that their experiences and ideological positions are the same as heterosexuals is unsupportable. But precisely where is the line drawn that divides the two sexualities? The range of political positions, both left and right, occupied by gay men, the prevalence of homophobia among gay men, and the "same sex" experiences of men self-identified as heterosexual makes any simple division impossible. To use the term *men,* in talking about males, is both unavoidable and too general. Similarly with *the body* or *women,* there is simply no easy solution given the limits of language. However, if these inaccuracies encourage a self-reflexivity, perhaps they, too, can be productive.

Intersubjectivity and the Individual

The theoretical tendency to reduce bodies to "the" body is inherent in metonymic uses of the term as well, such as the "social body" or "the body politic." The value of such tropes is that they allow us to perceive of large groups as organic entities by defining boundaries that frame structural investigations into social systems, and providing an understanding of various circulations. There are, however, difficulties with such figural uses of the body that are obscured by the apparent value of anthropomorphic gestures. First, a process of naturalization is put in place wherein hierarchies of high and low, the rational and irrational are imposed on the body and on culture, and reproduced through a system of mutual reflections. For example, certain classes are associated with "lower" bodily functions, while bodily functions are perceived as "dirty" like portions of society are deemed inferior. Each marginalization is used to justify the "reliability" of the other in a mirroring that obscures cultural ontologies in favor of biological assumptions of innateness.

Moreover, in figuring the body there is an underlying assumption that cultural forms are closed, self-contained systems. Sue-Ellen Case critiques this form of essentialism.

> What is essentialist, or at least metaphysical, the ruinous worm buried in essentialism, is the kind of argument that is ultimately based on a self-generating self referentiality, which has, in the eurocentric tradition, historically secured its closed status by an appeal to "ontology." In other words, what is structurally essentialist or metaphysical in an argument is the claim that the system rests, finally, on some self-generating principle—that it cuts loose from outside dependencies—operates outside of the historical, material conditions of change. (Case 1995a, 3)

The social body, like the human body, is seen as self-contained and isolated. Through this "inherent" aloneness are constructed ambivalent, if not oppositional, relations with other social or human bodies that are equally self-defined. The problem, as Case points out, is when the framing device is given ontological status, dehistoricizing the context that defines its usefulness as a trope. Despite the efforts of Foucault and others to describe genealogies of knowledge, there is a resistance to perceiving the body as anything but a discrete entity with a will sufficient to determining its own direction.

The existential image of a (male) body suspended between facticity and being, on an implacable trajectory between birth and death, in a predominantly hostile universe, has become, having lost its moorings in the desolation of postwar Europe, a cult of the individual. Issues of individual responsibility have been overwhelmed by visions of opportunity, and complicity in economies of destruction has been replaced by economies of consumption. This shift in the valuation of each person's unique qualities has followed two vectors. The first is the construction of an interiority. The directions and misdirections of psychoanalysis and the evolution of descriptive structures that allow for the identification of neuroses and psychoses have privileged the desire of *individuals* and the "right" to satisfaction. The second vector is toward an exteriority, defined by the need to individuate appearance, thereby confirming subjectivity, through the accumulation of property and wealth. The drive to establish an identity separate from those around us, even when acknowledged as impossible, serves to fuel a culture of consumerism and an insatiable desire for innovation. What is achieved is not coherence, but an increasing sense of fragmentation and an attendant loss of meaning in our lives—the inevitable end of individuation.

What is obscured in this overriding concern with the angst of self-disappearance, of nonsignification, is our dependence on intersubjective relations. The genius of marketing is that by appealing to a fantasy of individualism, the desire to belong, to be part of a group defined by outward appearances or normative behaviors, can be manipulated. This is possible because it is through interrelationships with others that we define an image of ourselves and, willingly or not, supply reflections in which others perceive themselves. Without the reinforcement of interactions, if only in memory, maintaining an identity is virtually, if not actually, impossible. And yet what we look for, and what we are encouraged to see, is individuality, that which separates us from others and devalues the significance of others in our lives.

Althusser, in his appropriation of Lacan, explores this phenomenon, albeit indirectly, through the concept of interpellation. Ideology is promulgated through acts of "hailing," in which a person is addressed and by responding positively embraces to a greater or lesser degree the values and relations proffered by the interpellator. In his description of this process, however, he abstracts an interpersonal interaction by attributing the act to an institution, claiming it is through macropolitical interpellations that dominant systems of values are reproduced in a society. Althusser acknowledges that hailings are frequently done by other people only to the extent that individuals represent certain relations to dominant ideological positions. He is less willing to accept that in many cases it is precisely interpersonal relationships, or the promise of human intercourse, that effects the interpellation into ideological positions. But the outlines of an identity are promised and provided by systems of reflection in the realm of the micropolitical, in the interactions between people; and the deciding factor in determining the strength of an ideological commitment is the intensity of the personal relationships. The power of the evangelical movement, the persistence of rock concerts, the development of "crash" clubs, and even the creation of alternative personalities on the Internet derive from the *need* for interpersonal interaction. And nowhere has the importance of relationships been more denigrated than in the ideologies of individualism.

And nowhere are the ideologies of individualism exemplified more persistently than in the defense of heterosexual masculinity. That men have been injured by an insistence on autonomy and a rugged individualism is now commonplace. But little has been done to address the ideological structures and the processes by which masculinity is constructed and the deleterious effects it has on intersubjective relationships. While questions of race, sexuality, class, and ethnicity have increased pressure on men to address issues of power and the distribution of resources, responses to these demands have focused primarily on macropolitical solutions and an investigation of social structures. Little has been done to theorize the micropolitics of masculinity. The deflection of this type of investigation is not surprising, because there is a very real threat to identity implicit in such an exploration. To question the basis of men's relationships with "others" is to open to scrutiny the structures with which men construct their lives. This book, in part, addresses that failure by examining the ways in which masculinity is figured and its effect on intersubjective relations.

However, to lay the problems of interpersonal relations at the feet of men is disingenuous, and not only because not all men are heterosexual. The structures of the body that construct desire and bear the inscriptions of social and cultural commerce are not absolutely dependent on determinations of sex or race. Complicity in systems of oppression and the constitution of differences between subjects that obstruct productive relations are frequently shared regardless of sex or gender, race or class. To explore, therefore, the ethics of intersubjectivity requires a willingness to look critically at ourselves as well as others. This is not to say that there are no differences. There are, and none more significant than the distribution of and access to power. The responsibility for effecting change and responding to structures of oppression do not fall equally. Those in positions of authority have the greatest responsibility for creating environments in which differences can be acknowledged and injustices reconciled. The greatest effects can occur only on the level of macropolitics, but without concomitant changes in the micropolitics of everyday relations, nothing will change.

This book, then, is an investigation of the body, of bodies, and the ways in which they interact. It explores the circulation of intensities within a field defined by the physical, the psychological, and the intellectual—in the spaces that define our differences and across which we strive to construct relationships. *Hearing Voices* is an ethics and politics of intersubjective relations that rests on the belief that only by improving the qualities of our communications can we begin to understand how best to reconstruct our relations with each other.

Chapter 2

Talking and
the Definition of Difference

In his correspondence with Jacques Riviere, Antonin Artaud seeks more than a validation of the poetry he feels compelled to write. Upholding the "truth" of the fragment, he is, most certainly, assaulting the bastion of conservative poetry, with its insistence on an aesthetics of unity. His refusal or inability to conform to the formal clarity Riviere expects to find in poetry is for Artaud both a success, marking the integrity of his work, and a failure, "the crystalline paralysis and pain of his mental apparatus as it tries to seize and formulate poetic imagery" (Barber 1993, 20). Artaud's conflict with language, his frustrations as he attempts to force it into forms that will contain the pulses of his creative thought, indicates more than an avant-garde rejection of established form or an insistence on poetry as the performance of the unconscious. It is an attempt to write in a way that will preserve his presence in his poetry; to keep himself from being lost in the proprieties of formal constructions. In addition to challenging aesthetic practices, Artaud seeks to open a literary space in which he can be recognized and *recognize himself.*

He believes Riviere's positive judgment will justify not only his continuing to write, but the very existence of his poems. "It is very important to me that the few manifestations of *spiritual* existence that I have been able to give myself not be regarded as inexistent because of the blotches and awkward expressions with which they are marred"

(Artaud 1965, 8). The poems for Artaud are not merely texts but living structures that embody the intensities of the writer. For the author the moment of objectification, when his product becomes alienated, no longer a possession but an artifact, has not taken place. His poems are proof that Antonin Artaud lives, and publishing them will prove he has "a mind that *literarily* exists" (Artaud 1965, 11). These "products of my mind" are extensions of his body and have the potential to validate Artaud's faith in himself. Artaud believes that publication by Riviere will restore confidence in his sanity, will bring to his mind "the concentration of its forces, the cohesion that it lacks, the constancy of its tension, the consistency of its own substance" (11).

Initially at least, Riviere fails to provide the understanding Artaud hopes to find. Instead of recognizing that the poems are the lifeblood of the author, he encourages the writer to rein in his temperament and to give the poems a more harmonic form:

> you do not, in general, achieve sufficient unity of impression. But I have enough experience in reading manuscripts to sense that it is not your temperament that prevents you from focusing your abilities upon a simple poetic object and that with a little patience you will succeed, even if only by the simple elimination of divergent images or features, in writing perfectly coherent and harmonious poems. (Artaud 1965, 9)

For Artaud the images are not "divergent," nor is he particularly interested in creating "coherent and harmonious poems." A series of anguished letters ensue in which Artaud struggles to communicate to Riviere the intensities of an unstable mind that make coherence impossible.

A turning point occurs when Riviere, finding a lucidity in Artaud's letters that is absent from the poems, suggests the possibility of publishing not the poetry but the correspondence. However, as editor he refuses to abandon his responsibility to publish what he believes to be good literature and suggests certain revisions—an interference that Artaud rejects—and the suppression of both his and Artaud's names as authors. Artaud fears the editing process will distort the truth he has tried to hammer out of language. He dreads discovering a fiction indistinguishable from the "formal excellence and . . . great purity of matter" typically published by Riviere in the *Nouvelle Revue Francaise* (Artaud 1965, 8). Artaud is afraid that if the publisher tampers with the correspondence he will cease to see himself in the work. "I won't let my thought be lost" (12). The fear of self-loss is also evident in his insistance that his name accompany the publication of the correspondence. They are not merely letters, but extensions of Artaud, his flesh.

The decision to publish the letters is marked by a shift in the tone of Artaud's writing. The desperate need to "signal through the flames" is replaced by a more temperate discussion of his condition.

> And there, sir, lies the entire problem: to have within oneself the inseparable reality and material clarity of a feeling, to have them to such a degree that the feeling cannot but express itself, to have a wealth of words and formal constructions which might join in the dance, might serve one's purpose—and at the very moment when the soul is about to organize its wealth, its discoveries, its revelation, at that unconscious moment when the thing is about to emanate, a higher and evil will attacks the soul like vitriol, attacks the word-and-image mass, attacks the mass of the feeling and leaves me panting as at the very door of life. (Artaud 1965, 21–22)

The images of the illness remain the same—the loss of the creative impulse, the disappearance of the self at the moment of materialization—but gone is the emphatic urgency to get Riviere's attention. Artaud is more certain that he is understood; he can now see the outlines of himself in their correspondence. He can say, as he never could before: "Enough about myself and about my works that are still unborn" (22).

There is a similar shift in Riviere's letters. Less time is spent attempting to analyze and minimize Artaud's condition; instead he tries to convey to Artaud the passions within himself, the fragility of his own mind that allow him to understand the other.

> I am not familiar with anything that resembles your "tornadoes," or that "evil will" which "attacks the soul and its powers of expression from without." But though the feeling I sometimes have of my own inferiority may be more general, less painful, it is no less clear. (Artaud 1965, 23)

A dialogue has begun between the two men. A conversation is made possible in part by the ability of each to comprehend in a relatively precise way the circumstances of the other. But more important is the belief that what they say is understood, that when Artaud receives a response from Riviere he will find himself reflected in that reply, that the part of him he can identify as his within the enunciation will be returned to him.

The relationship between Artaud and Riviere is mutually specular. The ability of each man to see himself in the words of the other is necessary for them to communicate. Only when Artaud perceives himself in the language and gestures of Riviere can he have confidence that he has connected with the editor. Similarly, Riviere can only speak about himself when, as the publisher of the letters, he can identify himself in relationship to Artaud and his writing. The implication is that the decision to publish signals the resolution of a difficult birth. What allows Riviere to make the offer are the interactions leading to the construction of a relationship that allows for mutual self-recognition.

Issues of specularity and context in the communication process are themes central to any discussion of intersubjectivity. Indeed, questions of who sees what and from where are as significant to the act of communication as what is said and how it is understood; the quality and efficacy of an interaction are, as with Artaud and Riviere, determined by how we position ourselves. It is from this perspective and this location that a discourse on talking and the difficulties of establishing self-reflective relationships in the reciprocal exchange of ideas can be engaged. Our conception of ourselves and where we stand, and the degree to which these are reinforced by the person to whom we are speaking, influences our interpretation of what others say and our definition of who they are. When communication breaks down, it is often because we can no longer see ourselves and, therefore, fail to see—perhaps a better word is *appreciate*—the person with whom we are talking.

Nowhere is this failure more evident than in communication across the boundaries of gender. The ways in which we position ourselves often makes mutually reflective conversation impossible. Despite a reputation for silence, men talk. When they do, instead of establishing a relationship of mutual reflection, they frequently rely on an already constructed self-image that demands a particular mode of response; and when they listen, they often listen only to the words relevant to that autorepresentation. Men, in particular, seem unwilling to serve as mirrored surfaces in which the people with whom they are engaged in conversation can see themselves; while, on the other hand, they insist that others serve that function for them: "In whose sight everything *outside* remains forever a condition making possible the image and the reproduction of the self" (Irigaray 1985, 136). If our expectations are not met, men (although not men alone) tend to stop talking, and indifference may set in, or violence, or self-doubt. The reciprocation necessary for productive communication depends primarily on how people with authority exercise their ability to control discourse.

Talking and Identity

Barry Champlain, the host of a call-in talk show in Eric Begosian's *Talk Radio,* loses control of his radio program and finds himself at a loss for words. I imagine him, in the silence that ensues, perched on the edge of an existential abyss in which fragments of his shattered identity disperse. But in that watching he realizes, suddenly or gradually, that he is not disappearing but is rather positioned on the edge of his identity. With that security "he smiles to himself" in celebration of his reconfigured self (Begosian 1988, 92). This recognition, this recentering the self, allows him once again to talk. "I guess we're stuck with each other" (92). The uncomfortable relationship described in this proclamation marks the distance he has traversed since the opening of the play, when he says, "I have a job to do and I'm gonna do it . . . and I need your help" (13). A barrier of distrust has risen between Champlain and the callers, who not only fuel the program, but provide him with the specular surfaces in which he can see himself.

Talking is important to Barry. He depends on his voice not only as a source of income, but more importantly because it is through speech that he defines himself. Like Artaud, whose words stand as a guarantee of his spiritual existence, Champlain's ability to talk is a sign that he is alive. "He lost his voice once in nineteen eighty-three. Freaked him the fuck out. At first he was climbing the walls . . . then he started getting depressed. . . . Real depressed" (Begosian 1988, 39). Language and the sound of his voice form one end of a dialectical binary; at the other is his conception of himself. Barry encounters who he is at the intersection of similarity and difference that lies between the two poles. The synthesis, insofar as one occurs, is located not so much in the knowledge he gains through the dialectic as in the solipsistic pleasure of experiencing himself.

But the materialization of the self in language is insufficient for both Artaud and Barry Champlain. Artaud seeks confirmation of his literary existence through Jacques Riviere and the publication of his poetry; Barry seeks it in interaction with the callers. People calling him approach the talk show host from a variety of perspectives that range from the inflammatory to the sycophantic: some wish to engage issues, some to receive approbation, some to get help with personal problems, some to denigrate him. The attitudes of the callers define positions to which Barry responds (if only to hang up) by constructing a position for himself that creates a tension with the self-representation of the person phoning. The images they project initiate a second dialectic between the talk show host and his guests in which each confronts the way s/he is perceived by the other. From Barry's perspective the relationship between himself and his callers is reciprocal. Both are allowed to assert their self-identity and, through his responses to their projections, are able to construct a synthesis that reinscribes or forces them to modify their image of themselves. The exchange would be mutual if they approached each other from the same point of view, but they do not. The callers are motivated by a need to express themselves; they have a certain investment in what they want to discuss. Champlain, on the other hand, is interested in the opportunity to improvise, because it is in articulating a response, rather than in the content of what is said, that he is able perceive the contours of who he is.

Because this is his objective, Barry does not feel constrained to present a consistent persona, but shapes himself to the contingencies of the moment, even if that results in holding contradictory positions. When Betty, a neo-Nazi sympathizer, calls to deny the reality of the Holocaust, Barry calls her one of "the bitter, bigoted people who hide behind anonymous phone calls full of hatred and poisonous bile" (Begosian 1988, 25). Later John, an African American, calls to praise Barry's stand against anti-Jewish prejudice, but instead of receiving approval for his position, finds himself attacked:

> don't you know how Jews feel about blacks? They hate you. You know those slums over on the East Side where the rats eat little babies for breakfast? Jews own those slums. . . . What do you mean "I like Jews." What are you, some kind of Uncle Tom? (40)

The degree to which the attack misrepresents John is of no importance to Barry because in shaping himself he has held up a mirror in which the caller can see himself and judge for himself the degree of distortion. Similarly, John's outrage at being called an Uncle Tom allows Champlain to evaluate the degree to which he has created the desired effect and to experience pleasure in his success. It is not merely a process of reinscribing a self-image, though this is often the effect; rather, Barry wants to be challenged, pushed to the point where a breakthrough is possible, where he surprises himself and is able to reconstruct his own image.

Within this desire there are traces of another agenda, a third dialectic. To be successful, Barry must engage the callers in a way that will also entertain the listening audience and meet their expectations of the program. The challenge of the improvisation lies in developing a dynamic structure of rising and falling tension through interaction with callers and the material they present him. His investment is not in the issues, but in the form of *Nighttalk*. The talk show host must oscillate between two poles. On the one hand, Barry must concern himself with how well he manipulates the callers; on the other, he needs to be aware of how his decisions affect the movement of the show. Barry must shift between choices that offer the immediate pleasures of engaging a caller and those that promise the deferred pleasures of successfully completing a program. It is in the synthesis arising from the fluctuating dynamics of now and later that he experiences himself.

The listeners are not the only audience of whom he must be aware. Champlain's being on the air is dependent upon the goodwill of his producer and the economic decisions of the sponsors. Barry actively resists acknowledging this reliance, embracing the belief that his show is an act of political subversion—an ideology he developed during the 1960s. Stu, Barry's engineer, remembers the days of "radical" radio.

> We thought we were changing the whole goddamn world right there in the studio. . . . He'd play "Let It Bleed" twenty-five times in a row just for the effect . . . or find a record with a particularly good skip on it and just let it go. . . . One time they had to knock the door down just to get Barry to take the record off. (Begosian 1988, 38–39)

But he knows, as he learned then, the relationship between outrageous behavior and success as a radio personality. "He didn't get fired, he got a raise" (39). Barry must create a dynamic rhythm that will not only keep his audience coming back, but keep *Nighttalk* on the air.

This triple dialectic defines the context in which the program depicted in the play takes place and provides the outlines of a theory of talking. Talking continually places us within the mechanisms of subjectivity that simultaneously defines our identity and charts the objectivity on which we project, and through which we explore, the validity of our self-definition. The processes of word selection and syntax not only define a specific expression, they also identify a subject position that we must decide whether or not we are willing to occupy. The choice to locate ourselves within a particular framework determines, at least for the duration of the expression, a relatively specific public image that requires an investment in the representation. Barry bargains that the person he sees reflected in the choices he makes will resemble him more or less precisely. Success, the synthesis of the dialectic, provides a degree of pleasure and a sense of well-being that derives from the act of reinscribing his identity. When Barry improvises the story of finding a Star of David on a visit to a concentration camp, he enjoys the image and his ability to imagine it.

> Who knows, it might have belonged to one of the prisoners of the camp, perhaps a small boy torn from his parents as they were dragged off to the slaughterhouse. . . . I kept that Star of David. . . . I know I shouldn't have, but I did. I keep it right here on my desk. (Begosian 1988, 25)

The truth-value of the tale is unimportant; what is significant is how he perceives himself at the moment of telling and the pleasure he experiences in defining himself as a subject.

This self-representation accompanies, becomes part of, the story as it is transmitted over the air and enters into the second dialectic. The reception of the now-public image by others and their responses will validate, or will not, Barry's pleasure. When Betty says, "Keep talkin', Jew boy. Life is short" and hangs up, Barry knows that his presentation of himself has had the desired effect. The conclusion of the process is not always positive.

CALLER: The question is obvious, why does an intelligent fellow like yourself spend so much energy hurting other people?

BARRY: People who love themselves are in love with a fool.
CALLER: Well put. Good night, Barry. (Begosian 1988, 84)

Barry has been finessed into seeing himself as other than he wants to see himself or to appear. His cleverness has led him to recognize an image of himself that displeases him, a process in which his self-image is put into question. Within these exchanges the model of the second dialectic appears less solipsistic because there is an assumption of reciprocity. Barry's interaction with Betty and the Caller creates a system of mutual reflections in which each can see how the other perceives them.

This model of equal relations among subjects assumes a level playing field and fails to take into account the effects of privilege and authority on intersubjective communication. Hierarchic relations allow one party to predetermine the contours of discursive exchange and to define a set of parameters for evaluating the return of the image. The boundaries of difference are already in place, and the possibility of reciprocal interaction is greatly diminished even before the callers are allowed on the air.

Champlain exploits this structure by creating situations in which the differences between himself and his callers are exacerbated. Champlain generally allows those who phone to initiate a topic of conversation. This issue establishes the parameters of discourse and severely diminishes their freedom to shift points of view. Barry further limits the space of interaction by adopting an antithetical, although not necessarily competitive, stance that determines a distance between the two parties. Callers must then decide how to advance their positions within this configuration. Regardless of the choice a particular caller makes, Barry's objective is the same: to control the conversation by maintaining tension, and by establishing a distance between the caller and himself. Therefore, his decisions have the effect of restricting his guests' ability to speak, of seeing themselves reflected within the discourse of talk radio. While the callers can be aggressive in attempting to dominate the interaction, they cannot "win," because they cannot silence him—he retains the power of the medium and, therefore, the privilege of having the last word. Even if a caller hangs up on him, Barry is still on the air. He can still talk.

This is particularly evident in his conversation with Rose, a single mother whose husband was killed two years earlier in a lawn mower accident. *Nighttalk* has become a means of relaxation after work and a source of comfort for her, distracting her from the noise of the children. Her grief, her job, and the children have made it impossible for her to establish a social life; and her call to Barry is an attempt to break through that isolation. Barry is "obviously bored by this call" (Begosian 1988, 61) but finds no acceptable way of disengaging her. Refusing to be drawn in by her offer of silk shirts purchased for her husband's birthday, Barry shifts the focus of the conversation and begins to weave a fantasy of his own. In a "sultry and whispery" voice, he begins to ask her what she is wearing. Rose, needing "someone special to talk to" (64), reluctantly answers his questions. Her children interrupt her; and Champlain, having been told she was alone, uses this "deception" as a means of ending the conversation.

When Rose calls she is responding to an invitation to enter Barry's world, which she accepts out of gratitude, an amorphous attraction, and the need for companionship. Barry is at first flattered by her call but soon finds that the conversation, *from his point of view,* is going nowhere. He is not getting what he needs, and he attempts to end the interaction, to usher her out of the mediated space they temporarily share. Unable to find suitable closure to the encounter, he reverses the relationship and, uninvited, begins to transgress the boundary that separates them. He enters into her world.

> Here we are talking on the phone, I've got my coffee and you've got yours. Two kindred souls sitting with our cups of coffee in the middle of the night. Alone together. . . . And I just, uh, was wondering what you were wearing. (63)

He shifts the focus of the call from the "neutral" space of conversation, as defined by the conventions of radio talk shows, to her personal domain. Her desire to expand her horizons, to engage in mutual dialogue, is resisted; and Champlain aggressively begins to limit her ability to pursue her objectives. He reduces her sphere of action by restricting possible topics of conversation, by talking. Her needs are overridden by his needs. He fetishizes her and then hangs up on her. "What a lovely woman you are, Rose . . . and me? I'm Barry Champlain" (65). He has supplanted her identity with his own. He can enact this transgression because he has the authority and privilege of altering the conversation to serve his own pleasure, and because there is another agenda to which he must attend, the dynamic of the program.

The demands of the radio show, the producers, and the sponsors determine to a large extent the choices Champlain makes. The pleasure he experiences through his interaction with the callers cannot be simply self-referential; rather, the response to his public image is placed in opposition to the expectations of those with the authority to take his show off the air. Barry resists the influence of the producer and advertisers, consciously attempting to disassociate himself from them. He refuses to submit to his producer's authority by bringing Kent, a disaffected youth, on the show live (70–71), and he denigrates the sponsors on the air. "Isn't that the most sickening ad copy you've ever heard? Harry's Restaurant? Home cooking? You ever go back into the kitchen of that place and you'd think you were in a taco stand in Tijuana!" (52). Nevertheless, he is cognizant of the fact that without them he loses the show, his ability to talk; without them he faces the same panic and depression that he experienced when he lost his voice. Barry must respond to their evaluation of the image he creates in his interaction with the callers.

The existence of an authority to which he is responsible other than that of the callers casts his on-air interactions in a different light. The public representation he creates and seeks to sustain on the program arises not only from his conception of who he is and how he likes to be perceived, but from his position in the institution of commercial radio and his belief in the medium as a "marvelous technology" (90). The satisfaction he receives from creating a good program is complemented by the approbation of the people he works with and for; similarly the experience of an unsettled self-image after a bad program is intensified by the displeasure of those with whom he identifies.

The communications through which we engage others and the self-images appended to public interactions are never simply self-referential but are determined by our investment in particular communities. It is in this context that Barry compares the representation of himself reflected back to him by his callers with the system of values on which he bases his identity and his position within the ideological structures of the radio station. Publicly, Barry denies any allegiance to the station because his individuality would be compromised by acknowledging the relationship and it might appear to contradict the image he projects of himself as provocateur. Therefore, Barry positions himself between the sponsors and his callers, believing a special empathy exists with those who telephone him and by denying his commitment to those who make the show possible. This location allows him to perceive himself as an individual dedicated to discourses of change and in opposition to institutions that reinforce the status quo. He is able to maintain this construction as long as the responses from the callers and his sponsors provide the pleasure necessary to sustain his self-image. Problems arise when the system of multiple reflection breaks down, when the callers refuse to return the image offered, insisting instead on defining the context in which they are to be seen. The effect on Champlain is devastating.

Barry loses control of the show and his ability to define himself in his interaction with Kent. Early in the evening, Barry receives a call from Kent, who claims his girlfriend has overdosed on drugs. Champlain understands the call to be the hoax that it is; and Kent quickly hangs up when his bluff is called. The sponsors, who are about to distribute the program nationally, fear the call may have been genuine and insist that Barry talk to Kent should he call back. The talk show host is outraged less by the challenge to his judgment than by their infringement upon his construction of the program. Kent does call back and is forced to admit the practical joke. Barry, having been proven right, decides to let Kent come down to the station in order to reassert his authority over the show, despite his producer's resistance. "Dan, this is *my* show. The sponsors bought *my* show. If I want to have this kid on my show, I'll have him on the show. I put who I want on my show" (71).

Kent arrives and Barry uses his awkwardness at being on the air to make a fool out of him, until he asks his guest how he and his friends respond to the "disturbing subjects" that are discussed on the program. Champlain is disconcerted when he learns that his listeners consider *Nighttalk* as entertainment, without any real social value. For the first, but not the last time, he is lost for words. Uncertain how to respond, he turns to the phones and begins to take calls; but he has become fixated on the question of the program's social value and his discovery that his callers take nothing from the show other than the pleasure of being entertained. Barry begins to recover from these unwanted reflections when Ralph, a neurotic, begins to list his paranoid fears. Champlain is about to deliver the coup de grâce when Kent shouts into the mike.

> You don't get it, wimp? Here's what you get: You get a dollar fifty-nine, go down to the drugstore, buy a pack of razor blades, and slash your fucking wrists, pinhead! (86)

Caught unaware by this parody of himself, Champlain calls for a commercial break and has Kent removed from the studio, but not before Kent whirls on Barry and blinds him with a camera flash at close range. His disorientation is deepened when the producer expresses pleasure at Barry's choice to bring Kent on the show

When he returns to the air, Barry holds all calls as he passionately defines the image he has of the show, and his position within that image. He then directs his attention to the audience, expressing his disappointment at their inability to rise to the occasion.

> I come up here every night and I make my case, I make my point.
> . . . I say what I believe in. I have to, I have no choice, you frighten
> me! I come up here every night and I tear into you, I abuse you, I
> insult you . . . and you just keep calling. Why do you keep coming
> back, what's wrong with you? I don't want to hear any more, I've
> had enough. Stop talking. (90)

However, he returns to the phone and asks them to talk; only this time he is in search of one person who understands what he means. Voice after voice speaks, only to be silenced when Champlain finds he is not hearing what he wants to hear; until Ralph, the man Kent told to cut his wrists, calls Barry with an invitation: "Come over if you want. . . . I have some cold cuts . . . beer. . . . Come over and we can talk some more" (91). "Barry stares at the mike. He starts to speak, but doesn't know what to say" (91). The silence grows, until Stu warns, "This is dead air, Barry, dead air." Having lost control of the show, Champlain takes his own advice and stops the talking, leaving forty-five seconds of radio silence. As he waits for the final seconds of the show to pass, "Barry realizes that he wants 'dead air.' He stares at the mike, smiles to himself, closes his eyes, waits." Once again in control of the show, he utters the final words, "I guess we're stuck with each other" (92). Barry recovers his composure and brings the show to a successful conclusion.

But there has been a disturbance in the field of play, and Barry must reassess his relationship with those in whom he sees himself reflected. A rift is created by the forty-five seconds of silence. Before the sequence of subversions that have undermined Champlain's sense of self, interchange between host and caller was based on an assumption of reciprocity, an equivalence of intensities with both parties actively engaged in the textual surface of the show: the concerns of the callers and the response of the host. With the revelation that the show is perceived by the listener merely as entertainment, there is a shift of the tectonic plates that define the program's structure. The ideological fabric that has mystified the talk show host is rent. An abyss is revealed across which Barry sees, for perhaps the first time, the outlines of his audience. He not only sees but hears them, and in that hearing recognizes his naïveté, his radically inadequate conception of the context in which he is working. In that epiphany, he experiences the disintegration of the self. The process of reassembling the fragments requires not only reconstruction of the self, but of his perception of the audience. No longer can they be "part of him, part of his mind." Instead they must be externalized, accepted as different. It is at this moment that a radical alternative is possible. As he experiences the effects of this existential upheaval, Barry has the opportunity to reconceive, in positive terms, his relationship to the audience. But the moment slips past; and where once they were allowed to talk, they are now silenced.

In refusing to hear them and instead embracing dead air, Barry redefines the boundaries that separate him from the audience. The previous limits have been transgressed, first by the producers who want Champlain to construct the program in a particular way, then by Kent, and finally by the callers who are unable to say what Barry wants to hear. The choice made by the talk show host is to insist upon the distance. Barry first uses the dead air as a barrier behind which he can recover from the loss of illusion—he is not changing people's way of conceiving the world—and then, as his new self-image solidifies, he lets the absence of sound become a gulf that only he can cross, because only he has the power to speak or to let them speak. Far from losing control over the show, Barry closes the program and resolves his existential crisis once again in a position of authority, once again defining the mechanisms of relationship. They have failed him. No longer is he willing to say: "I have a job to do and I'm gonna do it . . . and I need your help" (13); instead, he says: "I guess we're stuck with each other."

Into the initial structure of Barry's talk show, Kent inserts the carnivalesque. He successfully subverts the relations of power by inverting the hierarchies of privilege and mimicking authority. The system of discursive exchange is disrupted; and instead of perceiving himself as a social activist, Barry is forced to gaze into a different mirror in which he can only see an entertainer. Barry is unable to control the discourse, and in that loss of agency discovers the space of his subjectivity defined for him. The voices of his audience compel him to see distortions in his self-image and force him to understand that his identity is based on a misconception. The distance between his representation of himself and other's perception of him reveals a contradiction of immense proportions. As he is drawn into the festival of the other, as the callers take pleasure in seeing themselves, in talking, he experiences the trauma of marginalization, of being excluded from the community he thought he had defined. There is in this moment of separation a profound sense of isolation, of having the basis of his existence pulled out from under him.

In the sudden loss of self there lies the opportunity for a re-vision of his relationship with the people who call in and listen to his show every night. The paradigms he uses to classify the callers are put into question and open to redefinition. A new field opens in which to explore the relationships that bind and the differences that separate the world of the talk show host and the public. But the vertiginous spin of his existential crisis leaves Barry speechless; and in that silence, instead of perceiving the distinct subjectivities that make up his audience, he seeks himself. Failing to identify himself in their refusal to acquiesce to his vision of the world, Barry embraces a new cynicism that reinforces the boundaries of difference and ties him more tightly to the imaginary community in which he lives, the institution of radio. Repositioning ends the possibility of reconfiguring the host-guest relationships and returns him to the discourse of talk radio and the assumption of authority. His rejection of a radical alternative reveals the superficiality of his commitment to change and reinscribes his need to control discourse. The "dead air," the forty-five seconds of radio silence, marks conversion from a state of confusion to an act of power. Silence over the airwaves rapidly becomes oppressive, and Champlain's manipulation of the medium is an act of violence, of vengeance for the distress he has experienced. He reasserts his authority and once again positions them as the "other," as mirror in which he *will* see himself reflected.

A gap exists between the public image and the ideological foundations on which identity is based. But because we believe in the spontaneity of the voice, the distance is disavowed; and we hold, with the greatest integrity, that there is an absolute proximity between what we are and the truth we speak. But talking serves a function other than conveying, or not conveying, the truth. It gives us the opportunity for self-affirmation. Within the dialectic of subjectivity we attempt to prove the consistency of our self-representations. Achieving this guarantee requires limiting the mobility of the others in order that the speculum can continue and we can gaze upon our projected selves without distortion. The desire to justify our belief in a consistent identity necessitates controlling discourse and negating the voice of the "other" and, therefore, the potential for stumbling over contradictions. But as Luce Irigaray points out, "One sex is not entirely consumable by the other. There is always a remainder" (1993, 14). The remainder resists containment and insists on mobility, requiring us to engage in a play of meanings, to shift positions so that the mirror can be kept in "her" place. Contradiction becomes inevitable and acceptable as long as it can be sutured into the facade of who we are. Barry Champlain can call someone a bigot one moment and enact bigotry the next because it is *his* manipulation of images that defines who he is.

An existential crisis shatters the veneer of a consistent subjectivity, revealing the seams that attempt to deny contradiction. The integrity and the solidity of identity fragments. In that moment of disintegration, when what was once a coherent self fractures, exposing a void, we scramble for a foundation on which to construct a new subjectivity. At least this is the illusion we have. What this narrative fails to take into account is that we are already somewhere, watching. I do not wish to minimize the anxiety experienced in the moment identity crumbles, because it is precisely this pain and the *desire* for release that allows us to recognize the ground on which we are always already standing. This ground is the *imago* on which we construct a conception of ourselves, on which we "establish a relation between the organism and its reality,"

> which manufactures for the subject, caught up in the lure of spatial identification, the succession of phantasies that extends from a fragmented body-image to a form of its totality . . . to the assumption of the armour of an alienating identity, which will mark with its rigid structure the subject's entire mental development. (Lacan 1977, 4)

It is ideology, the cultural system of representations by which individuals define "not their real conditions of existence" but "their relations to those conditions of existence" (Althusser 1971, 164). This ground is not solid, however, but a tapestry of the imaginary, woven of the combined affects of voices we have heard and forgotten, but which are ingrained in the body by experience—the traumatic as well as the everyday. It, too, is subject to disruptions. But as long as nihilism, in its most precise definition, is avoided, there remains a matrix of beliefs that constitute the subject and define our relationship to the external world, making possible the renewal of identity.

From this position we begin, once again, to promulgate an image of who we are. But there is a difference. We must find a new audience against which to identify ourselves. The collapse of identity arises when those on whom we depend to return images of ourselves refuse to fulfill that function. Their insistence upon independence, on living within the remainder, denies us access to the representations we offer as evidence of who we are. What they experience as an expression of self, becomes for the subject in authority a dangerous negativity. To escape the implicit critique, we find ourselves allied with another community, one defined by our transformed understanding of our relation to our context. It is not a new population, but one in which we have already been interpellated and whose values we have incorporated into the fabric of our bodies. For Barry Champlain that community is defined by the medium of radio. He may be stuck with his listeners, but he continues to identify with his colleagues. "As he passes Stu's desk, he slaps his hand as he did when he arrived at the top of the show" (Begosian 1988, 92). The pleasure in that slap of the hand cements an old relationship newly valued. The callers will be there when *Nighttalk* returns, but Barry will approach them differently. The boundaries of difference have been raised; he will not use the medium to engage them in an act of subversion. They are no longer part of his mind. Rather, they exist out there, and he will take greater pleasure in defining their otherness. Nothing has changed; there is merely a new inflection to his talk.

But the possibility of change offered itself for an instant. There was a brief moment when Barry could have asked what concerns his callers have, when he could have allowed them to see their cares reflected in him. But that would have maintained the disequilibrium he suffered. *Nighttalk* would have a new purpose based on issues of significance to the community. The danger, of course, is that it would not work, that the sponsors might abandon the program and Barry Champlain would have to stop talking. Barry decides not to defer the construction and promulgation of a public image until a new relationship with his audience can be conceived; he chooses not to risk the insecurity of change.

He opts, as most of us would, for the comfort of an identity that leaves the authority and privilege of his position intact. He remains in control of the program by constructing boundaries of exclusion that mark a shift in his affective investments from faith in his audience to the commercial venture of radio. The need for security in self is stronger than the desire for change.

The point I wish to make is not that Begosian should have written a different ending to the play, or that Barry Champlain should be condemned for his actions, but to observe, as I shall throughout the book, that the radical or liberal impulse to change, particularly with people in positions of authority, tends to yield before the pleasures of a secure image of the self. The investments made in visions of the future depend on the ability to reinscribe representations of self, and if that concept of the self should fail in the glare of an unflattering reflection, the desire for change recedes. In its place arise boundaries of difference that marginalize while celebrating the world within the walls, the community of the same.

Talking is a means of communication, but it is also the means by which lines of difference are drawn and communities of inclusion are formed. Talking initiates a dialectic of specularities that has the potential for developing mutual understanding, but that all too often is used to reinscribe systems of belief grounded in the negation of the other. In the heart this discourse circulates the question Luce Irigaray addresses specifically to men. "But what if the 'object' started to speak? Which also means beginning to 'see,' etc. What disaggregation of the subject would that entail?" (1985, 135). It is an unresolved question with profound implications, and one that refuses to go unanswered. If Champlain's response to the destabilizing critique of identity is in any way typical, what hope is there that we can be instrumental in effecting change? We shall return to this question time and again in search of a strategy that will not end in the negation of the other but in a dismantling of the boundaries of marginalization, a resistance to the desire to deny difference in the name of the same.

Artaud and Riviere perceive in each other a quality each lacks in himself. Artaud sees in Riviere the ability to validate the materialized contents of the soul; through the act of publication Riviere can guarantee the value of Artaud's existence. The editor lacks the turbulence that drives Artaud, that opens vistas of creation beyond inferiority. But this reciprocity is not evident until Riviere opens a space in which the two writers can enter into a process of mutual reflection, in which each can open himself to one another, in which they can be two men talking. But this is possible only by resistance. Artaud uses his letters to transgress and limit Riviere's freedom to define a discourse. The poet insists on talking only of his poems and his impossible relationship to their perfection. The editor resists this all-consuming desire until he is able to shift the discourse by opening the field to include their correspondence. Suddenly there exists a body of work in which both can experience and talk about themselves with respect for each other's difference.

This is not necessarily as optimistic as it may sound. By reframing the context in which the discussions between the two men take place, there appears to be an increase in the *potential* for empathy—the ability to equate our own experiences with those of another and to appreciate the similarities. This does not imply a diminishing of differences, however, but a shift in perspective that may conceal continuing resistance. Riviere has not agreed to publish Artaud's poetry, suggesting a continuing antipathy to fragmentation. Artaud has succeeded in getting published, recognized as existing, but not in the form he believes most conducive to his creative energies. In forging a compromise, the editor maintains, at least in his own mind, his responsibility to the publishers and his reading community. Not forced to the extreme of "dead air," Riviere nonetheless maintains his allegiance to a particular ideological position and thereby secures his relationship with that community. Therefore, while boundaries are refigured in ways that can be construed as positive, it does not necessarily mean that change has occurred in either man's subjective relation to the context in which he moves.

When in *Talk Radio* Betty says to Champlain, "Keep talkin', Jew boy. Life is short," her ethnic epithet is both a denigration and a performative. Champlain is brought into existence as Jewish, not for the talk show host but for the like-minded listeners who define Betty's community. The fact that those for whom her statement is felicitous are absent is insignificant. Betty knows—regardless of how illusory—that she acts on behalf of a larger constituency, and that her statement, regardless of how derogatory, will substantiate their beliefs. Similarly, if only in this respect, Riviere performs on behalf of an absent community and can believe—again however illusory—that his decision to publish the letters will be seen as felicitous, regardless of Artaud's response. Artaud, as well, may have seen the publication of his correspondence as a victory, by way of example, for the surrealists; or he may have believed that Riviere's decision creates a context that includes him as member of the editor's community. In short, what seems a sharing, an opening of boundaries, may actually be the reinscription of differences. What is positive, regardless of these possible constructions, is the ability for each to share their insecurities with each other across the space of difference. Nothing may have changed, but understanding may have increased.

But this is in the realm of the same or, from Irigaray, of hom(m)osexuality. Is such dialogue possible across the boundaries of sex and gender? Would this reconciliation have been possible if one of them had been a woman? These are not idle questions, but issues that must be addressed if we are to understand the micropolitics of intersubjectivity.

Chapter 3

Reinscribing Difference

Talking is used to define boundaries of difference. Those limits are important because they confirm our identity, not as individuals but as intersubjective beings with links to a particular community that supports an image of ourselves. When a disintegration of the self occurs because of a conflict that throws into question our relationship to those with whom we identify, the pain of that existential crisis is experienced as an internal wounding, the opening of an abyss. Its resolution, when a resolution is possible, involves establishing connections with people whose values and behaviors allow us to recognize ourselves, once again, as valued persons. The fact that we can realign ourselves and commit to a new image of self indicates the tenuousness of identity and our ability to reimagine who we are. Such a recovery does not imply the construction of a *new* identity, but a reformulation of self based on existing patterns of being (see chap. 5). The injury caused by such an experience encourages us to cement relationships within the community that enhances our sense of self, and to reinforce the boundaries of difference that separate us from those who threaten—however illusory the threat—to disrupt our sense of identity.

The discourse of intersubjectivity is based, to a large extent, on spatial relationships. Conceptualizing boundaries, individual subjectivities, and communities involves the translation of differences into distances and territories. This chapter will look at how space and territorial divisions, both literal and figurative, are used in relationships to define and more importantly maintain identities and therefore differences. The focus of this investigation is gender, specifically the relationship between feminism and the "men's movement," which seeks to reconcile differences through sensitizing men. In a reading of Sam Shepard's *A Lie of the Mind*—a play seen by some women as feminist—I will show that the text, through the disposition of spatial relationships, echoes certain ideologies implicit in the recent men's movement. Rather than addressing a feminist agenda, it reinscribes, however unintentionally, boundaries of difference.

> They understand that many men feel that they have lost the ability to claim their manhood in a world without fathers, without frontiers, without manly creative work. (Kimmel 1993, 51)

The pressures of feminist politics that threatened the walls of patriarchal privilege in the late sixties and early seventies were met with a variety of responses from men that ranged from attempts to strengthen the ramparts of difference to calls for opening the gates; from the "moral majority"'s insistence on keeping women in "their place" to efforts by men to advance profeminist agendas. The impact of the women's movement was powerful and immediate, but it was not until the 1980s that men began to organize nationally as a means of responding to feminism. Again, male response was varied, but generally fell into two main camps: "men's rights advocates—those struggling to extend the rights of men—and pro-feminist/anti-sexist men—those struggling to end the violence men perpetrate against women" (Thorne-Finch 1992, 204). The general public was made aware of the "men's movement" when the poet Robert Bly began holding conferences, specifically for men, designed to address the effects of feminism on masculine identity. A PBS special, "A Gathering of Men," and Bly's book, *Iron John*, at the end of the decade gave national prominence to "new age men." The mythopoetic movement—as it is also, and perhaps more appropriately, named—has as its stated objective helping men to overcome the "feminization" of masculinity, perceived by Bly as a negative effect of feminism, without losing sensitivity to the legitimate claims made by women (Bly 1990, 2–4). The response by feminists and profeminists has been highly critical of Bly's position and will be discussed later.

Profeminist men in academia became more vocal in their

responses to the discourses of feminism during the 1980s. One of the notable and perhaps notorious events was the 1984 MLA panel "Men in Feminism," where, in the first of two sessions, Paul Smith, Stephen Heath, and Andrew Ross defined their positions as profeminist men. In the second session, Alice Jardine, Judith Mayne, Elizabeth Weed, and Peggy Kamuf raised problems with these locations, focusing primarily, but not solely, on the invasive implications of the session's title. Generally the position of the women was that men do not belong in feminism, if for no other reason than feminism is not about men. It is, fundamentally, about women defining and expressing themselves as they move from under the dominance of men. The intensity of the dialogue continued beyond the convention and resulted in 1987 in a collection of essays that included the original conference papers, *Men in Feminism*, edited by Paul Smith and Alice Jardine. The decade also witnessed a concerted effort by some academics to introduce men's studies into the curriculum as a necessary counterpart to women's studies. The debate found its way onto the pages of *The Chronicle for Higher Education*, where Harry Brod called for a "new field" of men's studies, as a complement to women's studies (Brod 1990, B2–3), while others argued against the concept as both unnecessary and detrimental to women's studies, since it would create competition for scarce resources (Wheeler 1990; Strange 1990).

The issue of men and feminism surfaced in popular culture as well. Dustin Hoffman, in *Tootsie*, portrayed a man who gains sensitivity by passing as a woman but is successful only because he exerts veiled male power, implying "that women must be taught by men how to win their rights" (Showalter 1987, 123). In *Tightrope* (1984), Clint Eastwood's character, Block, is brought into contact with feminism, which "becomes a principle of law and order" that "allows a reshuffling of the polarities of desire and violence" and, ultimately, gives voice to a "desire for a heterosexual relationship where the transgression of boundaries can be pondered without losing one's self" (Mayne 1987, 67, 70). The "new man" also began to appear on television, as husbands in the most traditional relationships attempted to be more sensitive to the needs of their wives. Most notably John Goodman in *Roseanne* portrays a traditional working-class man who takes an active part in the problems of raising children, discusses marital and financial problems openly, and supports Roseanne's efforts to maintain her own identity.

The engagement of men with feminism also found a voice in the theater and nowhere more contentiously than in the plays of Sam Shepard. A playwright who had been roundly criticized for valorizing oppressive male violence suddenly found himself recuperated by some feminists who found in *A Lie of the Mind*, specifically, a profeminist play. Recently Janet V. Haedicke defended the play by locating in the postmodern, decentered subjectivity of the characters "[n]o 'sanctification of powerlessness' but the voice of power[;] such truth creates in the cultural theater that discourse in a 'democratic political space' which constitutes a feminist politics beyond *ressentiment*" (1993, 91). She locates in the theater an image of women empowered, and the possibility of a dialogue beyond negativity in which an equality exists between all participants. The advent of central female characters who seek, and some would say find, agency in Shepard's narratives encouraged the belief that, in *A Lie of the Mind*, the playwright was perceiving "the world from the point of view of women as opposed to superimposing a male view on history" (Rosen 1993, 6). Shepard, however, is more reticent about claiming allegiance with feminism, locating its influence in "a period of time when there was a kind of awareness happening about the female side of things. Not necessarily women but just the female force in nature becoming interesting to people." For him what is of interest is "how that female thing relates to being a man" (6). If we take Shepard at his word, then instead of a profeminist agenda, he was interested in pursuing the effects of feminism, or the consciousness feminism helped to create, on men, that is, exploring masculinity and its discontents.

It is from this perspective that I will approach *A Lie of the Mind*, as an attempt to define masculinity in a world disrupted by feminist discourses. The play, I will argue, is Shepard's response to a particular historical moment in which, like many other men, he felt the need to confront the implications of feminism for masculinity. In this context, and because of Shepard's interest in dysfunctional myths, I contend that *A Lie of the Mind* demonstrates an affinity with Robert Bly's mythopoetic men's movement and is, therefore, subject to the same critique.

Shepard resists the realistic form in *A Lie of the Mind*, disrupting the action with seeming non sequiturs and iconic moments that gain ritual or symbolic significance through a transformative aesthetic. The American flag that appears throughout the play can be read alternatively as a symbol for the dead father, as a piece of clothing, as a cloth for wrapping a gun, and finally as an image of the American family of which proper care must be taken. Similarly, the struggle between Baylor and Frankie for the blanket that Jake ultimately wears when he leaves the Montana house can be understood variously as a source of warmth, a death shroud, a symbol of territorial power, an alternative to the significations of the flag, a cloak of sorrow indicating the isolation experienced by the existential man, and the mantle of patriarchy. The dialogue of the mimetic narrative is also subject to disjunctive juxtapositions, perhaps most clearly when Mike brings Jake into the house. Proud that he has captured the family's "enemy," Mike is surprised to find that while Beth becomes fixated on Jake and Frankie proclaims his innocence, Baylor scolds him for mistreating the flag, ultimately dismissing his son and folding the flag with Meg.

MIKE: Beth, you get back here!
BAYLOR: *(Referring to rifle)* What're you doin' with that?
MIKE: Dad, I've got the bastard right outside on his knees. He's agreed to make an apology to the whole family. Where's Mom?
BAYLOR: Never mind that. What're you doin' with that rifle? What's that wrapped around it?
MIKE: It's just a flag. He had it on him. He had it all wrapped around him. I wanted Beth to come out so he could—
BAYLOR: *(Pause. Taking a step toward Mike, kicking blanket away)* It's not just a flag. That's the flag of our nation.
(Shepard 1986, 115–16)

These formal devices create an unstable dramatic surface that precludes satisfaction of conventional expectations of narratological and psychological verisimilitude.

This style of writing has led critics to think the play postmodern. For Haedicke, for instance, the use of floating signifiers to which multiple meanings can be attached is a decentering strategy. She perceives within this mode of writing a "chaotic multiplicity" that resists the desire for unity by rejecting modernist "subjectivity by opposition and subjugation by gender for one of subjectivity in difference and connection in contradiction" (1993, 92). Rosemarie Bank also considers *A Lie of the Mind* "decidedly postmodern" (1989, 227).

Self becomes Other and multiplies, displacing spaces of representation and creating a heterotopia that transforms continuously because in *A Lie of the Mind* there is no single rupture [threshold] of history. . . . Here, memory is fractured from the play's beginning, like Beth's battered mind, fragments floating and mocking the idea of a single relationship that could be called truth. (Bank 1989, 237)

Gary Grant, on the other hand, taking the same perspective as Haedicke's and Bank's, that is, the image of a post-Heisenberg universe, perceives in Shepard's dramaturgy a high-modernist impulse.

> His playwriting method violently probes at the surface, fragmented appearance of acts and attitudes and objects, as it seeks to reveal the mysterious reality of wholeness beneath. Shepard's complex juxtaposition of theatrical images carries the dynamics of this belief not as a concept or an epistemic sign, but as a living image of this ever-changing wholeness. (Grant 1993, 128)

Shepard seems to position himself in terms of the latter, exploring a "world behind the form" (Shepard 1977, 53), where the "great hope is that it moves into something that is true" (Rosen 1993, 3). He does seek closure, but a form that "leaves you on the next note . . . cycled. So that you go through something that you are really returning to; that place you began" (Rosen 1993, 6). Shepard's desire for a return to origins and for an authentic truth also lends credence to Lynda Hart's evaluation of Shepard's dramaturgy. She finds that his family plays are "essentially" realistic because "the characters are searching for an identity that is gradually revealed through dialogue and action; . . . dialogue alternates between concealment and revelation; recognition scenes uncover a secret that explains the main character's problems," despite Shepard's "distinctive deviance from this realistic pattern" (Hart 1989, 218). To perceive the play as fundamentally modernist necessitates a reconceptualization of the function of the form.

Grant believes Shepard's style of writing reflects the playwright's interest in music rather than a postmodern sensibility.

> Similar to the rapid transitions in jazz and the simultaneous word/music thinking of rock 'n' roll, the experience of Shepard's discontinuous dramaturgical design gives a sense of sudden liberation, a sense of flow, of play, of freedom from time and space limits, a sense of sudden growing transformation. (1993, 122)

If we read the form as a jazz structure, *A Lie of the Mind* presents characters who, seemingly independent of the others on stage, "improvise" on a particular theme before returning to the organizing principle of the music, that is, to the narrative.[1] The effect is to keep the audience focused on the fractured surface, while implying that the whole is greater than its parts. The tendency for characters to go off on tangents apparently irrelevant to what is occurring (Baylor is more concerned about his mules than his daughter's health) and for them to deny relationships between people (Meg forgets/denies that Beth and Jake are married) does not discount an underlying unity so much as draw attention to those moments of convergence when reciprocal communication occurs and the intensity of the characters reveals the emotional geography Shepard is exploring. "Not effect so much, it's territory, emotional territory. I'm interested in effects only to the extent that they serve some purpose, some purpose of emotional terrain" (Rosen 1993, 3). When Sally tells Lorraine of Jake's complicity in the death of his father, or when Jake meets Beth in the final scene, there occurs a moment of contact between the characters that reveals the powerful emotional intensity of their interpersonal relationships, placing them in bold relief against the montage of contradictory and transformative representations that defines the landscape of *A Lie of the Mind*. In this context the fragments, while creating postmodern effects, conform to modernist strategies and suggest that we should locate Shepard next to playwrights such as Harold Pinter rather than Heiner Müller.

This disjunctive musical structure works in tandem with the organization of the stage space in foregrounding the theme of displacement, in the mythic sense of American homelessness. Set in the West, the two families live at opposite ends of the country: Jake's family in Southern California, Beth's in Montana. The distance between the two families is geographically reinforced by the Rocky Mountains and deserts that separate the two states, and metaphorically spanned by the marriage of Jake and Beth. Placing the play primarily in the two homesteads creates two concrete locations represented side by side on the stage, between which is an undefined, liminal space.

FRANKIE: Okay, okay. Take it easy. Where are you then?
JAKE: Highway 2.
FRANKIE: What state?

JAKE: Some state. I don't know. They're all the same up here.
    (Shepard 1986, 3–4)

Haedicke and Bank, in their discussions of the setting, privilege the discrete "home" locations. For Haedicke, "On each side of the stage is
enacted an Oedipal scenario, which mimics the theatricality inherent in
the cultural construction of gender roles" (1993, 87). The "middle neutral space" that separates the two locations functions primarily to render "concrete the binary construction of gender" (87); but she does not
understand this space as particularly significant, in and of itself. Bank
grants greater significance to the "in between," perceiving it as the
locus of the dead. "While Jake's ultimate trajectory . . . is outside and
dead, Beth's is interior and alive" (Bank 1989, 233). There is evidence to
support this engendering binary. It is in this liminal space that Jake has
beaten Beth to the point of death, and from which he is brought home.
It is in this undefined distance that Mike locates the badly battered Beth
unable to speak and walk, and where her family comes to take her to
Montana, where she begins to recover. These readings serve to position
the critics who want to recuperate the play to serve a certain feminist
agenda. However, Hart, writing from a feminist perspective less sympathetic to Shepard, cites Jurij Lotman to support her contention that
the use of space reinscribes male privilege within traditional gender
differentiations.

> Characters can be divided into those who are mobile, who enjoy
> freedom with regard to plot-space, who can change their place in
> the structure of the artistic world and cross the frontier, . . . and
> those who are immobile, who represent, in fact, a function of this
> space. (Hart 1989, 221)

Lorraine and Sally in Southern California and Beth and Meg in Montana may rule within the home, but this does not guarantee them narratological agency. Instead, according to Lotman and Hart, they serve
to define the qualities of the landscape represented by each, while the
men, as agents, advance the story through their mobility. The divisions
of the stage are no less engendered, but there is a definite shift in the
configurations of power and authority from the view presented by
Hart to that of Bank.
    Women who enter the liminal space between the two locations put

themselves at risk or are unable to define a trajectory for themselves. Beth is, once again, beaten when she attempts to construct a life for herself outside territory prescribed as "female," and she almost loses her life. Once back in the family home and asked to step out on the porch, she refuses, and Mike attempts to force her across the threshold. "DADDY! HE'S TRYING TO TAKE ME AWAY! DADDY! . . . He's trying to take me outside. I don't wanna go outside now" (Shepard 1986, 115). Similarly, Sally considers going to Montana but cannot bring herself to do it.

SALLY: I was just—I was driving around the house. In circles. Real
        slow. I couldn't make up my mind.
JAKE: No, I mean where were you headed originally? Before you
        decided to come back?
SALLY: I wasn't sure. I mean—I was thinkin' I'd go up and try to see
        Beth, and then . . . (Shepard 1986, 56–57)

She is unable to enter, let alone cross, the distance that separates the two families. When she does leave with Lorraine, the "traditional gender roles" do not "reverse as Lorraine and Sally . . . penetrate the 'out there'" (Bank 1989, 237) because although they traverse liminal spaces, they are returning to a matrilineal heritage, to Lorraine's family, to "Mary Skellig" (Shepard 1986, 110), to the landscape of women.

Men, however, seem to have no trouble passing through these distances. Jake, Frankie, Baylor, and Mike all travel the West without apparent difficulty. Instead, it is within the home that the men feel most uncomfortable. Jake feels imprisoned by his mother and seeks to escape; Baylor and Mike take turns living in the hunting shack, a male domain located on the boundaries of the "women's" territory; and Frankie spends most of the play trying to get out of the Montana house. Jake's father left home for Mexico, living just across the border, and Baylor wishes he was out in the mountains. "I could be up in the wild country huntin' antelope. I could be raising a string a' pack mules back up in there. Doin' somethin' useful" (Shepard 1986, 99–100). Significantly, it is into the space between that Jake disappears at the end of the play—the frontier of male subjectivity.

This division of space is reinforced by the designation of the home as the site where women live and have authority. Lorraine puts Jake in the room he had as a child and reverts to being a nurturing and punishing mother. Preparing for him his childhood favorite, cream of broccoli soup, she insists: "I'm gonna take him on a permanent basis. I'm not even gonna let him outa his room for a solid year. Maybe that'll teach him" (Shepard 1986, 25). Lorraine's "smother-love" is reserved for the men in the family, however. When Sally threatens to leave because her mother brings Jake, a man who beats women, home, Lorraine's response is concise: "Then leave, girl. This is my boy here" (26). Sally does not leave but helps Jake to escape from what has become a prison for him.

SALLY: You better go through the bathroom window. She'll see you if
    you try to cross the porch.
JAKE: I know how to escape. Don't worry. (79)

It is a place women control, and from which men leave.[2]
    The site that marks the end of Jake's flight from home is no less "matriarchal." Baylor seldom sets foot in the house, preferring to spend his time in the hunting shack, a place untrammeled by female presence; and when he does come home, he seldom leaves the living room. Similarly, when Frankie is shot or when Mike enters the house, both are confined to the downstairs. Upstairs the bedrooms belong to the women; and for a man to be upstairs is to be privileged.

    We got an extra bedroom empty don't we? Let's just move him up
    there. Then we can serve him breakfast in bed. We can move the
    TV up there for him. How 'bout that? We can get the electric blan-
    ket. He could even share the room with Beth, maybe. That'd be
    nice and cozy. (Shepard 1986, 50)

Frankie is never given that privilege but is, rather, consigned to the couch.
    The engendering of space, while it reflects the administration of public spaces in the United States, is not done simply to reinforce gender constructs, "the woman's place is in the home," although this is a side effect of Shepard's choice. The two houses locate the women in the play in order to isolate and create a parallel between their trajectories.[3] This structure encourages the reader to contrast their stories while also differentiating what is for Shepard the more important journey, that of Jake—with whom, I believe, he identifies deeply, but with great con-

sternation. To understand the implications of Jake's movements, however, we need first to look at the women.

Lorraine and Sally are diametrically opposed in their attitudes toward Jake at the beginning of the play. Sally perceives him as persona non grata, as a man who abuses women, and opposes bringing him home. Precisely what she expects her mother to do is never articulated, except in the negative: she does not want him in the house. This is, in part, because of his violence, but also because of his tendency to perceive reality in terms of conspiracies and lies. When Jake returns home, he attempts to make an ally of Sally.

JAKE: *(Whisper)* She's with him, Her and Frankie are together. They've got a pact.
SALLY: What're you talkin' about?
JAKE: . . . Are you with them too?
SALLY: I'm not with anybody, all right! I'm all by myself.
JAKE: Then you can help me. There's no reason why you couldn't help me. (Shepard 1986, 59)

Sally tells her mother about Jake's conspiracy theory, making Jake feel betrayed and turning Lorraine against her daughter.

LORRAINE: Well—looks like you're just gonna have to stay away for a spell, Sally. We can't have him gettin' upset like this. Not in his condition. He wasn't like this until you showed up.
SALLY: *(Still with her eyes on Jake)* I'm not leavin'. I'm sick to death of leavin'. Every time I pack, I tremble now. I start to tremble. It's in my body. My whole body shakes from the memory of all this leavin'. It feels like a leaving that will last forever. This is my home as much as his. (62)

Her resistance to Lorraine arises from a fear of external spaces and from her need to establish herself as a daughter within the family. To secure her place within the home and to help Jake get out of a situation in which he feels a prisoner, Sally helps him to escape.

Lorraine attacks Sally for helping Jake get away, accusing her of trying to destroy the family. "It's you that wants to undermine this entire family! Drag us down one by one until there's no one left but you" (90). Sally denies the allegation and insists Lorraine realize that her life has revolved around men. Lorraine eventually admits that her husband is "still alive in me. . . . He's still walkin' around inside me. He put stuff into me that'll never go away" (86). It is only by breaking trust with Jake and telling Lorraine of his complicity in the death of their father that Sally is able to draw a parallel between the two men and convince her mother that, as women, they need not be caught in a world defined by male competitiveness and insecurity.

> I'm sick of being locked up in this room. In our own house. Look at this room. What're we doin' here? This was Jake's room when he was a kid. What're we doin' in this room now? What're we sup-posed to be hiding from? (90–91)

Recognizing her position within the house and within the discourse of patriarchal authority, Lorraine is jolted into an awareness of how she has been trapped, how she has become a prisoner in the house she thought was hers.

This epiphany allows Lorraine to see how constrained her life has been because of the demands placed on her by the men in her family.

> All the junk in this house that they left behind for me to save. It's all goin'. . . . They never wanted it anyway. They had no intention of ever comin' back here to pick it up. That was just a dream of theirs. It never meant a thing to them. They dreamed it up just to keep me on the hook. (91)

The relationship between the women undergoes a radical shift, and Sally and Lorraine together yearn for one "a' them fierce, hot, dry winds that come from deep out in the desert and rip the trees apart. You know, those winds that wipe everything clean and leave the sky without a cloud" (91). They create their own desert wind and systemat-ically go through all their belongings, destroying anything that links them to the past. Setting fire to the house and all its contents, they pre-pare for a new life in Ireland, where they will attempt to make contact with Lorraine's family, reestablishing links to other women.

Sally and Lorraine's journey is a movement out from under the domination of men, a breaking of links with the past and the beginning of a new story—a story of women together. This profeminist moment is tainted, however, because, as in the work of most male playwrights, when women are together and not talking about men they are occluded from the frame of representation. Once the men have ceased to exist in their lives, it seems impossible for Shepard to imagine a mother-daughter relationship, and he has no choice but to have them leave the stage. His decision may be honest, a recognition that as a man he cannot understand, let alone represent, how women act when they are not focused on men; or, less sympathetically, it may be convenient, for once they are gone he can complete the narrative with which he began—the story of Frankie and Jake (Rosen 1993, 7). Nonetheless, these menless women are never heard from or mentioned again.

Beth and Meg tell a different story; one that allows them to remain on stage, within the frame of representation. It begins with a difficult birth or, more precisely, rebirth. Beth must learn once again to walk and talk as she struggles back from the damaging effects of Jake's beating. The process of recovery and the interpretations given to the "new" Beth have become pivotal in feminist recuperations of *A Lie of the Mind*. Haedicke and Bank focus on the significance of her fragmented speech, because within her stutterings there are the outlines of an intelligent and perceptive woman capable of a critique of masculinity.

> Look how big a man is. So big. He scares himself. His shirt scares him. He puts his scary shirt on so it won't scare himself. He can't see it when it's on him. Now he thinks it's him. (Shepard 1986, 70)

She is also capable of a vision of future relationships: "You could be better. Better man. Maybe. Without hate" (72). Haedicke, particularly, embraces the pronouncements of Beth, which she believes "suggests agency within mediated subjectivity" (Haedicke 1993, 90). Beth as a nascent female subject resonates for Haedicke with Donna Haraway's call for situated knowledges and Nancy Love's advocacy of vocal metaphors as a site for "a political transformation. . . . an empowerment/knowledge regime" (Haedicke 1993, 91). Haedicke envisions within this construct a time when "wives no longer weep in Oedipus's house" (91). Bank also perceives Beth's recovery as a transformative process wherein a definition of subjectivity lies, found not in the characters as individuals but as representatives of a geography that defines "a landscape of the mind": "[the play] could be said to fragment single selves into their component and warring parts" (1989, 232). The value of this perspective, for Bank, is that it allows us to read *A Lie of the Mind* as a subversion of gender because it "provokes us to explore the set of relations inside of which we live because we are both the subject and object of gender analysis" (239). These interpretations are certainly provocative and bespeak an intense desire to revise relationships in a way that opens the possibility of a reconstruction, if not dissolution, of traditional gender definitions. There exists within the readings of Haedicke and Bank resonances with Judith Butler's theory of performativity and the troubling of gender. Beth's active seduction of Frankie does subvert a specific construction of femininity, but unlike Butler's search for new paradigms, there is a precedent for Shepard's alternative.

Beth was beaten while she was rehearsing the role of Maggie in *Cat on a Hot Tin Roof*, "all about how she's bound and determined to get this guy back in the sack with her after all these years he's been ignoring her. How she still loves him even though he hates her. How she's saving her body up for him and him only" (Shepard 1986, 10). Coincidentally, at least in the fiction of *A Lie of the Mind*, her family situation parallels that of Maggie in Tennessee Williams's play.[4] Baylor as patriarch attempts to control events through belligerence and sarcasm, in much the same way Big Daddy does. He is not to be contradicted; Meg even feels it necessary to ask permission to stay near her daughter in the hospital. Big Daddy's domain is the land; Baylor spends most of his time in the hunting shack from which he can survey his property. But when he is at home, he expects his needs to take precedence. "All right. All right! Stop rubbing my feet now. Go on upstairs! Go on. I've heard enough a' this" (Shepard 1986, 99). Meg's self-reliance and control over interior spaces allows her to witness, as Big Momma does, what appears to be the rebirth of her family. Beth nurtures her relationship with Frankie: "I wanted to keep him warm" (Shepard 1986, 118); while Baylor, having successfully folded the flag in military fashion, intimates a returning intimacy.

MEG: I believe that's the first time you've kissed me in twenty years.
BAYLOR: Aw, come on, it ain't been that long. Let's go on up to bed
     now. (122)

There is a reaffirmation—however illusory—of the "traditional" American family, the belief that the home and family are the source of meaning, if not happiness. This ideology is shared by both Big Momma and Meg.

Mike parodies Goober, the self-centered big brother who strives to discredit Brick and gain the inheritance of the estate. Similarly, Shepard's character attempts to humiliate Jake and keep Frankie from assuming a proprietary position in the household. "You wormed your way in, didn't you? Pretty cute. But I'm not forgettin' anything. Everybody else might forget but I'm not. As far as I'm concerned you and your brother are the same person" (Shepard 1986, 51). Finally, Frankie, like Brick, has an injured leg and spends most of the play keeping Beth at a distance, resisting her seductions.

Beth, using the model she has rehearsed with such intensity, locates an identity that gives her a grasp on reality to which she can cling. Replaying the role, she lavishes all her attention on Frankie in an attempt to gain his love, despite his resistance. Like Maggie, Beth tries to lure Frankie into bed, projecting onto him Brick's homoerotic tendencies. "You could pretend to be in love with me. With my shirt. You love my shirt. This shirt is a man to you. You are my beautiful woman. You lie down" (Shepard 1986, 71). She is undaunted by his refusal and continues to woo him, attempting to locate in her body the woman she thinks Jake/men want. To this end, Beth imitates Maggie's techniques of seduction by dressing, as Williams's character does for Big Daddy's birthday party, in clothes that accentuate her sexuality and are designed to arouse Frankie. "Beth is dressed in a bizarre combination of clothing. She wears black high heels with short woolen bobby socks, a tight pink skirt—below the knees, straight out of the fifties—a fuzzy turquoise-blue short-sleeved, low-cut sweater, green tights" (Shepard 1986, 104). In *A Lie of the Mind*, however, her costume reenacts the confusions of adolescence—bobby socks and low-cut sweaters—perhaps indicating a stage in Beth's recovery, and/or a parody of contradictory images of femininity. Whether we accept these interpretations or accept Haedicke's reading of this moment as subversive, Beth believes she can overcome all obstacles and achieve a revitalized marriage based on love, which in Shepard's play seems possible through Frankie, as in Williams's play it ultimately seems possible for Maggie through Brick.

> You could be better. Better man. Maybe. Without hate. You could be my sweet man. You could. Pretend to be. Try. My sweetest man. . . . You could pretend so much that you start thinking this is me.

You could really fall in love with me. How would that be? In a love
we never knew. (Shepard 1986, 72)

It is in the desire for a sweet love, a true love, that Shepard locates "the
female side of things. Not necessarily women but just the female force
in nature" (Rosen 1993, 6). "The female—the female one needs—the
other" (Shepard 1986, 98). It is in Beth; it is in Maggie the Cat; and both
of these women seek their "natural" identity in relation to their men.

Beth hopes, through this trajectory, to experience the love she was
unable to have with Jake because he lacks faith. It is as though she were
attempting to make Frankie into the Jake she wanted to love—that is,
someone who trusts and cares for her without jealousy and violence.
But there is a cost exacted by this desire. Beth is no longer interested in
seeking a career; she has lost, at least within the limits of the play, the
drive to define for herself an independent existence outside of the
house. Locating herself inside the home gives Beth self-assurance, a
confidence her mother also experiences. It is to this world, in *A Lie of the
Mind,* that men gravitate.

If there is a "female" side of things, there must also be a "male"
side; another force in nature to complete the binary. The ideologies of
the American dream are generated and regenerated by a mythical bal-
ancing within this gendered equation. Frankie and Jake leave their
fatherless home, the domain of an obsessive mother (at least from their
perspective). What is lacking in Lorraine's house is the force of "masculine rationality" that Baylor provides his family. "Let her do it. She
can do it. 'Bout time she starts doin' things by herself. You keep babyin'
her she's never gonna get any better" (Shepard 1986, 51). A home without a father, without a patriarch, is a place from which to escape, particularly if you are a man.

But Shepard seems to find within this configuration another "lie of
the mind," because the home is also where Mike developed into the
stereotypical figure of masculine competitiveness and narcissism. He
tries to emulate Baylor by becoming a hunter, but the two men do it for
very different reasons. Neither do it to provide food; but Baylor perceives hunting as something men do because it defines who they are:
"Hunting is no hobby. It's an art. It's a way a' life" (Shepard 1986, 96).
It's "what you do" if you are a man and it is hunting season. For Mike
hunting is a way of proving he is a man, the equal of his father. "Tell
Dad I kept the rack for myself. It's a trophy buck. He can have the meat

but I'm keepin' the rack" (75). Mike, by killing the deer, has, according to his definition of masculinity, entered the ranks of men and is ready to assume responsibility for protecting the family, a function Baylor has failed to accomplish, in his opinion.

Mike's vision of what it means to be male is of epic proportions and is based on media images of the frontier and the need to defend "the women" from marauders. He achieves the status of hero by "capturing" Jake and beating him into submission.

> He'll confess to us. I broke him down good. You shoulda seen him. He was crawlin'. I just kept him on his knees. I kept him there. You shoulda seen it, Dad. Every time he'd try to stand up, I'd knock him back down. Just hammer him down until he gave up completely. He gave himself up to me. He's my prisoner now. (Shepard 1986, 106)

Masculinity, within this framework, is defined as the ability to completely humiliate an opponent, to force him to surrender his life to the victor. Mike is appalled to discover that no one cares. "So it doesn't make any difference, is that it? None of it makes any difference? My sister can get her brains knocked out and it doesn't make a goddamn bit a' difference to anyone in this family!" (117). Instead of being recognized as a savior, Mike is forced to see that his "Rambo" mentality is superfluous, that it may be a hindrance to the well-being of the traditional American family rather than its saving grace. "It's not just a flag. That's the flag of our nation. Isn't that the flag of our nation wrapped around that rifle? . . . What do you think you're doing, using the American flag like a grease rag" (116–17). "Patriotism" is not to be confused with militarism, but located in the family, to be protected by giving it the proper respect.

There is, however, another movement taking place in *A Lie of the Mind;* a trajectory for which the discourses on the "true" man and the "ideal" family serve as a landscape. Jake's journey is put in sharp relief by this 1980s reenactment of *A Cat on a Hot Tin Roof* and the elision of women without men from the field of representation. The two sides of the stage become screens rather than mirrors, where Jake sees not his reflection but modes of existence in which he can no longer invest. He cannot live in either but must seek a geography with positive contours in which he can play out his masculinity and its discontents.

You know, in yourself, that the female part of one's self as a man is, for the most part, battered and beaten up and kicked to shit just like some women in relationships. That men batter their own female part to their own detriment. (Rosen 1993, 6)

Jake has had his "feminine" self battered and becomes a distorted figure defined by negative features. He is a man who abuses women because he is unable to believe they can love him or be true to him. The beating of Beth that opens the play is not the first instance of wife abuse, but one in a series of incidents. "There was other times when you said you'd killed her—when you thought you'd killed her—remember?" (Shepard 1986, 57). Violence has become part of his life, and while it is not only directed toward women, he blames them when he loses his temper.

JAKE: I done my time for her. I already done my time.
FRANKIE: She had nothin' to do with that. She never did.
JAKE: She got me in trouble more'n once. She did it on purpose too. Always flirtin' around. Always carryin' on. (13)

The lack of trust that marks his relationship with Beth is only one facet of a more general paranoia. He perceives conspiracies around every turn. His mother imprisons him in his room; Beth has landed him in jail (82); and Sally conspires with Lorraine and Frankie, who is trying to take Beth from him.

JAKE: I want Sally here, where I can see her. Where I can keep an eye on her. She's not gonna be sending any messages for you anymore.
LORRAINE: Messages?
JAKE: Yeah, that's right. You can tell Frankie that she's not coming back there. She's staying with me. There's not gonna be any more codes sent. (63)

His alienation from all around him forces him to seek an alliance with Sally against his mother and to protect, irrationally, his room and bed, which he claims as his territory (32).

His paranoia, possessiveness, and irreconcilable jealousy exacerbate the isolation he experiences, his sense of desperation at having lost Beth.

Now. Why now? Why am I missing her now, Frankie? Why not then? When she was there? Why am I afraid I'm gonna lose her when she's already gone? And this fear—this fear swarms through me—floods my whole body till there's nothing left. Nothing left of me. And then it turns— It turns to a fear for my whole life. Like my whole life is lost from losing her. Gone. That I'll die like this. Lost. Just lost. (15)

It is the hollowness he feels that must be confronted. The journey he takes to reconcile himself with this emptiness in the core of his being is manifested not in the discourse of language but through images—a trajectory that begins with a return from the liminal spaces of the Western landscape, where he beats Beth, to the room he had as a child and the ashes of his father.

Jake seeks to escape the aimlessness and violence of his adulthood by going into hiding, by surrounding himself with the objects of his childhood and the women who raised him. Instead of finding solace, he becomes feverish and pale as he grapples with the implications of loss and his culpability as the murderer of Beth. The process of reconciling himself to his actions is complicated by his involvement in the death of his father, which, if Sally is to be believed, was tantamount to murder. His resistance to acknowledging his complicity is signified metaphorically by draping the American flag around his shoulders. To wrap oneself in the flag is to be immersed in patriotism, in the mythology of natural innocence, of national perfectibility. To reject this innocence, to recognize the impossibility of staying within the bosom of his family, requires that Jake confront his ghosts. Shepard does not make Jake address his complicity in the death of his father; that is left to Sally, who recounts the events in Mexico, the precipitous collapse of male camaraderie. "At first it was like this brotherhood they'd just remembered. But then it started to shift. After about the fourth double shot it started to go in a whole different direction. . . . There was a meanness that started to come outa both of them like these hidden snakes" (Shepard 1986, 87). The love between father and son disintegrates into a hatred that manifests itself in competition, the need to prove oneself better, more male. The need to destroy the other becomes an act of vengeance, as if through the humiliation of the father Jake will be able to heal those parts of himself that have been "battered and beaten up and kicked to shit," those wounds within himself created by his father's absence. "Jake murdered him! And he never even looked back. He was already sitting in some bar down the road ordering the next round of drinks. He never even got up when he heard the sirens" (89). It is only when he returns home that he must look back, that he must open the box that contains his father's ashes and come to terms with his death. "He blows lightly into the box, sending a soft puff of ashes up into the beam of the spotlight" (39).

Jake's relationship to his father has to be confronted because he needs to recognize the violence within him that led to his beating Beth. The process he undertakes is again shrouded in feverish silence and is not narrated by Sally this time. Instead it reveals itself in two short speeches. The first occurs as he resists looking into his violence.

> Don't think about her feet or her calves or her knees or her thighs or her hips or her waist or her ribs or her tits or her armpits or her shoulders or her neck or her face or her eyes or her hair or her lips. Especially not her lips. Don't think about any of these things. You'll be much better off. (Shepard 1986, 55)

In a state of denial, he attempts to obliterate her memory, to keep from imaging her as she was before and, perhaps, after his violence. His image of Beth is as a fragmented physical being, an erotic object that conjures sensual memories, but not as a sexual object—her primary sex organs are not mentioned, she has no vagina—nor as a thinking person. She has no identity as an individual; rather, as a fetish, he idolizes in her absence. The other speech occurs when he confronts Beth, after he has escaped from home, from Mother and Sally, and crossed the distance that separates the two domiciles.

The change in his attitude is signaled through the resignification of the flag. Before leaving he wrapped himself in the flag as a form of protection, as a means of denying his complicity in his own acts of violence. Upon arriving in Montana he is "captured" by Mike, who uses the flag as reins on a horse and a gag. The stars and stripes meant to shield him become a form of bondage that constrains him from expressing himself. Jake's humiliation at Mike's hands, replicating the humiliation he inflicted on his father, brings his story full circle. He has lost his claim to innocence and must recognize how this pose has trapped him, kept him from seeing who he has become, from seeing what Beth means to him. "I—I—I— I love you more than this earth" (Shepard

1986, 118). It is through this unremitting love that Jake is able to perceive the lies in his mind.

> These things—in my head—lie to me. Everything lies. Tells me a story. Everything in me lies. But you. You stay. You are true. I know you now. You are true. I love you more than this life. (120)

Beth has become a beacon that can pierce the layers of anger and paranoia, of mendacity and self-absorption, and shed light on the man who has been beaten beyond recognition, who has denied the "femininity" within himself. She reveals to him an aspect of himself that can love without violence. But he also knows he cannot trust himself, that he will hurt her again—that his being there is at best destabilizing to her, at worst promises another act of violence. When he "leans towards Beth and kisses her softly on the forehead" and she "pulls back" (121), he understands there is no hope of reconciliation, of another chance. He forgets about the flag, wraps the blanket around himself, and leaves, having told Beth: "You stay with him. He's my brother" (120). There is no destination. His home has been burned, and his mother and sister have left the country; he has no occupation we know of to which to return. There is only the liminal space, the mountains and deserts of the West, the onetime frontier, in which to lose himself. It is perhaps he that Meg speaks of when she utters the final words of the play. "Looks like a fire in the snow. How could that be?" (122).

I have read the end of *A Lie of the Mind*, the conclusion of Jake's journey, as sympathetically as possible because I believe this kind of an interpretation would be necessary to make the text work in the theater, which it did, winning for the playwright the New York Drama Critics Circle Award for best play of the year. It is also an attempt to evoke the intensity involved in what is for Shepard a "move into a certain kind of emotional terrain" in order to find in the play "something that is true," "true to itself," "something that is its own feature" (Rosen 1993, 3). This landscape is difficult to explore because it continually shifts underfoot and resists being caught in the languages of representation; and to hazard such an investigation in search of the gestures that can convey what for the playwright and the characters is true, however that is construed, requires the greatest integrity. But no playwright can write outside of their own experience, outside certain habits of thought and ways of perceiving the world that define their relationship to the community in which they live. This is not to denigrate the imagination, but to recognize that what is perceived to be true is based on local ideologies rather than transcendent universals; and to find the truth is to reveal the contours of socially constructed systems of belief rather than to provide access to a set of metaphysical absolutes. To be critical of the play in terms of images of masculinity is not to be critical of Shepard or to question the intensity of his investigations, but to reveal the contours in which he writes and the ideologies that determine the images of men.

When Jake leaves at the end of *A Lie of the Mind,* he has been transformed from a man who beats his wife senseless to an existential anti-hero, a "fire in the snow." Indeed, the fact that he has almost killed Beth recedes during the course of the play until it is all but forgotten, sublimated within images of an impossible love, lost in Beth's gradual recovery and return to lucidity. Similarly, we forget Jake's history of wife abuse and cease to wonder what the juridical implications of his criminal behavior will be; the inevitability of her recovery seems to render such questions unimportant. The torment he experiences, his guilt and his loss, are supposed to be punishment enough. To perceive the text in such terms is, however, to rip it from its context and place it immediately in relation to the quotidian; an act few plays could endure. Shepard is not writing realism, but seeks to find his forms in the interplay of myth and everyday experience, an exploration of how the architecture of one informs our understanding of the other in a movement of reciprocal reflection. It is in the disjunctions and compatibilities between the highly structured and seemingly accidental that the possibility of meaning begins to appear. *A Lie of the Mind* explores the tropes that define and are defined by a certain emotional landscape, the boundaries of difference between men and women in relation to images of American family life.

Jake's violence, within this framework, is a complex metaphor that signifies the intolerable distance between hegemonic images of men and women placed within a context of dysfunctional families and feminism as an emerging "awareness . . . about the female side of things" (Rosen 1993, 6). Jake seems incapable of accepting Beth's independence within their marriage. Her movement out of the home and into the traditionally male workplace threatens his security as a male because he links the choice to work with sexual liberation. Failing to understand her profession or her approach to acting, he misreads the empowerment she feels as a working actress as an indication of her dissatisfaction with him; a solipsism exacerbated by her refusal to take his jealousy seriously. "And she laughs. Right to my face. She laughs" (Shepard 1986, 9). Seen both as a sign of contempt for his feelings and a brazen denial of sexual infidelity, he reasserts his authority through the only means available to him: physical violence. This is, of course, a "lie of the mind" and, ultimately, is the one he must overcome if he is to complete his journey.

His inability to reconcile himself to Beth's career, her movement into an "open" space, creates a fissure in his life, represented by Lorraine's and Sally's gradual movement away from him. These women come to understand the narcissism of men. Used as pawns in an elaborate game of conspiracies, first in the relationship between father and son—Sally is made complicit in the death of their father when she witnesses the accident that kills him—and then in the matrix of Jake's paranoia, the two women extricate themselves from the landscape of masculine manipulation and begin to construct new lives between themselves in which there is no room for a male presence. While this action opens new horizons for the women (literally and figuratively, they go to Ireland), it deprives Jake of his childhood—he can no longer return home. Jake finds equally impossible a return to Beth, who has lost, or is now afraid to express, the vibrancy that defined her empowered independence. Instead, her energies are condensed into the creation, or re-creation, of a relationship within the structures of the nuclear family, which locates women's self-identity within the home, where they have a modicum of authority, but where they are expected to recognize that the desires of the father take precedence over their own needs.

These worlds carry decidedly different valences for men. The rise of feminism and tendencies to separatism, at least in its early stages, excluded men, much as women had been excluded from men's clubs. Insisting on a space free from male interference, women set about the task of rediscovering their history and articulating a vision of their future while confronting the effects of their liberation and the pressures exerted by men for inclusion. Barriers, understandable and necessary, were established so that women could undertake the painful and difficult process of self-discovery and, in some instances, self-invention. Other women, those who resisted the feminist movement, invested themselves more completely in the family, continuing to define themselves in terms of male desire and traditional structures that feminists identified as a primary source of male oppression. Far from being excluded, within this framework men are necessary and, at least in Shepard's play, are seduced into acceding to the limits of family life.

The family, however, is seen by men as a trap. Baylor has spent most of his life in the hunting shack, a male preserve within the family, in order to find the space in which "to be male." Mike takes over this edifice in an attempt to reexert patriarchal authority in a family that has become dominated by women. Frankie also resists becoming incorporated into the family structure, spending most of the play trying to get out of the house—partly out of dread of Jake, but also out of fear of Beth, who has decided how he should live his life. The only thing that keeps the men in the house is that they are crippled—Frankie has been shot and Baylor is unable to walk. The implication is that they will leave when they are able or, in terms of Freudian imagery, that they are castrated and therefore impotent when within the house run by women. Indeed, when Jake enters the house Beth exclaims, "THERE'S A MAN IN HERE! HE'S IN OUR HOUSE!" (Shepard 1986, 120), implying that on some level, Baylor and Frankie, who are also in the house, are less than men.

By kissing Beth, Jake gives his blessing to her choice and sanctions the family by accepting Frankie as his replacement in Beth's affections; but it is an option that he rejects for himself. Jake, the "man," walks out into the snow, replaying the many Westerns in which John Wayne or similar men ride off, letting go of the woman they love because they know their love is impossible. Unable to live within the confines of the family and excluded from the world of women together, he is homeless, forced to live in the liminal space between two unacceptable options. "The male one goes off by himself. Leaves. He needs something else. But he doesn't know what it is. He doesn't really know what he needs. So he ends up dead. By himself" (Shepard 1986, 98). This, at least, is how Meg sees it.

Stepping out into this space, Jake is also reenacting his father's leaving. There is no explanation given for his father's desertion of the family; just the implication that he cannot live with his wife in the confines of familial life. Like so many men in Shepard's plays, Jake's father goes to Mexico, a border that opens onto vast expanses of desert, a frontier that marks the margins of the United States, a semipermeable membrane through which illegal migrations flow. It is in Mexico that he is

able to stop drinking and establish a possible, if rudimentary and isolated, existence, outside of the juridical and familial administration of
his existence—that is, until his family returns and he loses his life.

For Jake, finding his father is a rite of passage, the need to demonstrate both his difference from and his superiority to the patriarch.
Mike undergoes a similar ritual by killing the trophy stag and leaving
the mutilated carcass for his father to dress. Ironically, this initiation
into manhood, designed to demonstrate difference and separation,
ensures the continuation of the patrilineal line, a repetition—the one
form of identity Jake absolutely rejects.

SALLY: Only because you remind me of Dad sometimes.
JAKE: Dad? *(Pause)* Dad?
SALLY: Yeah. You do. Sometimes you sound just like him.
JAKE: I don't sound anything like him. I never sounded like him.
  I've made a point not to. (Shepard 1986, 60)

Jake *is* different. Unlike his father, he does not just disappear; instead
he goes to see Beth one more time and to express his love. Nonetheless,
he walks away from marriage and family to construct his own life, outside the confines of territory administered by women, in a liminal
space, on the frontier.

In constructing this image of self-marginalization, Shepard gives voice
to the experience of many men who recognize their fathers in themselves and, therefore, must acknowledge their complicity in women's
oppression; who are sufficiently profeminist to reject the traditional
matrices of marriage and family but are unable to conceive an alternative relationship, so ingrained is the voice of the father in their lives.
The effect is an existential crisis revolving around the impossibility of
finding a place where they can be in relation to women. It is not coinci-
dental that the men's movement has arisen to address the reality of this
crisis, nor should it be surprising that the therapeutic model involves
men retreating from women and family, going into the woods, literally
or metaphorically, in an attempt to reconnect with the essential masculinity within them and to overcome, through reconciliation, the
wounds inflicted by the fathers (and mothers) on their sons.

Robert Bly, a founder of the "mythopoetic" movement, perceives
the process of healing as the rediscovery of a masculinity that mediates

the distances between the hard, nonshuddering man—the savage—
and the "new" man, the "soft" man, who is

> life-preserving but not exactly life-giving. . . . Here we have a finely
> tuned young man, ecologically superior to his father, sympathetic
> to the whole harmony of the universe, yet he himself has little
> vitality to offer. (Bly 1990, 3)

What Bly seeks to recover for men is the mythic archetypal identity of
Iron John, the Wild Man, a creature distinctly different from the savage.
"The savage mode does great damage to soul, earth, and humankind.
. . . The Wild Man, who has examined his wound, resembles a Zen
priest, a shaman, or a woodsman more than a savage" (Bly 1990, x). The
Wild Man resides in all men, in the liminal spaces between consciousness and unconsciousness, outside of society but in sympathy with its
"civilizing" qualities. To embrace the wild man within himself, the man
must leave the mother's world, where he has "lived happily since
birth," and find his way to the father's world "which naturally seems to
them dangerous, unsteady, and full of unknowns" (86). The man who
has embraced the Iron John within is "open to new visions of what a
man is or could be" (ix).

Shepard has not, of course, reached the peak of optimism Bly has
obtained, nor do I wish to suggest Shepard would in anyway support
the mythopoetic movement. There are, however, within the work of the
two writers strong parallels in the stories they tell. Mike can be perceived as the dark side of men and their "mad exploitation of earth
resources, devaluation and humiliation of women, and obsession with
tribal warfare" (Bly 1990, ix); while Frankie is "soft," "more thoughtful,
more gentle . . . a nice boy who pleases not only his mother but also the
young woman he is living with" (Bly 1990, 2). Jake seeks another
course, away from the savageness that led to the beating of Beth, but
one that remains "hard." To do so he must embrace the ashes, not only
of his father, but the death of his childhood. "Job covered himself with
ashes to say that the earlier comfortable Job was dead; and that the living Job mourned the dead Job" (Bly 1990, 81). He escapes the mother's
world and bids farewell to Beth, before entering the uncertain and
unknown world of his father. What Shepard and Bly recognize and
express, through similar interests in myths and shamanism, is the
malaise of late-twentieth-century masculinity, the feeling that men

"have lost their ability to claim their manhood in a world without fathers, without frontiers, without manly creative work" (Kimmel 1993, 50). Or, more specifically in Shepard, the manhood they claim is violent and aggressive, or dependent and helpless.

Both Shepard and Bly want to reclaim what they perceive to be a lost male heritage. Shepard wants to rescue the feminine side of men from the battering and abuse it experiences in attempting to meet the impossible standards set by the hegemonic discourses on masculinity. Bly also wants to rescue men from dominant images of what it means to be a man, *but also* from the effects of the "feminized" man. Each of these men depends on a double set of binaries. The first is that of sexual difference. Men are biologically defined as different from women, creating an absolute distance between them. The criteria used by men in making this distinction are based on primary and secondary sexual differences, and it is assumed the same criteria have been adopted by women. This binary is continually reinforced by a distortion: although we use the plural in referencing sexual difference, our definitions are based on the singular, most commonly the images in biology textbooks that show clinically and graphically the physiological differences between a man and a woman. The second or subsidiary duality is based on the analogue that conflates sex and gender: male equals masculine, female equals feminine. While the standards for defining gender are not as absolute, they are nonetheless perceived as marking clear and distinct differences based on the binary of male and female. Women and men are categorized according to their proximity to one pole or the other, insisting upon a point of demarcation, an either-or, identical to that used to differentiate the sexes.

The terrain these men are exploring is defined by a dual axis, north-south as male-female, and east-west as feminine-masculine. Where these two lines would cross there is not a point of intersection but a void, a no-man's-land (but possibly a woman's land?), a space of liminality, of neither-nor. However, they do not explore this unpopulated space, perhaps out of fear that what will be found is not a connection but another distance between points, a third axis dissolving the binary into a field of differences. Instead, Shepard and Bly retreat to the uncontested pole of the male in search of a new definition of what has become for them an outmoded conceptualization of the masculine. The nature of the exploration further distorts the original dual axis, because in the move to the male, in order to define its relationship to the female,

Shepard and Bly appropriate the feminine pole of the gender axis for their discussion of what it means to male/masculine. What is elided from the discussion in this move is any consideration of the female, of women. In other words, what arose as a problem between the sexes becomes a crisis for masculinity to be addressed by men among men— or individually, alone on the frontier.[5] As a result, women are marginalized, and their voices are not heard. They are either absented from the frame of representation or are presented in negative images as dominatrices who trap men in feminine structures that are emasculating or drive them to violence.

If the voices of women who are loved—mothers, sisters, wives— are not heard, to whom do we listen in this search for a new masculinity that will allow us to create a new and vital relationship to women? Ultimately it is the voice of the father, whether it has been passed down in the myths of patriarchy, like Iron John, or as Vince describes in Shepard's *Buried Child:*

> I could see myself in the windshield. My face. My eyes. I studied my face. Studied everything about it. As though I was looking at another man. As though I could see his whole race behind him. . . . I saw him dead and alive at the same time. In the same breath. . . . And then his face changed. His face became his father's face. Same bones. Same eyes. Same nose. Same breath. And his father's face changed to his Grandfather's face. And it went on like that. Changing. Clear on back to faces I'd never seen before but still recognized. Still recognized the bones underneath. The eyes. The breath. The mouth. (Shepard 1981, 130)

What we discover when we seek answers in the world of men, unheeding the voices of women, is always and already imprinted with the name of the father, by the history of men, which has been largely the history of oppression and exploitation: a masculinity in which violence to women becomes acceptable as a metaphor for savage male behavior, and forgivable if the woman recovers; an act in which the woman disappears, becoming a mirror in which men see themselves. What they seek in that reflection, what may appear to be a new synthesis, a new vision of what it means to be a man—regardless of the purity of intent—will carry with it the "Same bones. Same eyes. Same nose. Same breath."

What Shepard's characters seek is not a new vision, but a revision, a rereading of masculinity in traditionally male terms, but inflected by feminist criticism. It is a lie of the mind, because the play does not open spaces in which women can explore themselves as subjects, but a calculation, once again, of what women want in a man—that is, what is good for men. The ruse upon which this articulation is founded is that of essentialism. Like cultural feminism, Shepard and Bly assume there is *a* masculinity that has been distorted over time and that can be healed through a return to the Father, through a shedding of the layers of affect that conceal the true masculine, which includes men's "female" side: "it became interesting from that angle: as a man what is it like to embrace the female part of yourself that you historically damaged" (Rosen 1993, 6–7). The move is a comforting one, because it allows men to stage a quest, the ontological search for the ur-male. It is a journey into an interiority where a balance is sought between "inherent" violence and the ability to love. Unfortunately, in both Bly and Shepard the reconciliation is not between men and women, but between men and their fathers, men and themselves.

Similarly in both Shepard and Bly, this movement of self-discovery is contingent upon a move away from "civilization." In seeking to contact a damaged self, men seek "healing" by crossing a threshold and entering a liminal space. "The passage from one social status to another is often accompanied by a parallel passage in space, a geographical movement from one place to another" (Turner 1982, 25). Jake's disappearance into the liminal space between the two homes, the frontier, and Bly's taking groups of men into the woods, or secluded encampments, mirror the change in social status that takes place, in this case from being a damaged to a "more whole" person. The major differences are that one travels alone and the other organizes groups; and while Jake's fate is uncertain, the men who attend Bly's meetings return home, however transformed. As Victor Turner points out, this movement "may be likened to loops in a linear progression, when the social flow bends back on itself, in a way does violence to its own development, meanders inverts, perhaps lies to itself, and puts everything so to speak into the subjunctive mood as well as the reflexive voice (1988, 25). This exploration of potentials creates the possibility of new understandings "as these are culturally defined" and, "in order to raise them to a higher rung of some structural ladder, inwardly transformed to match their outward elevation" (26). The movement from one space to another, the division between liminal and factual spaces, is not designed to be disruptive, but to validate existing social structures, to make the interior reflective of the exterior. For those who already dominate in relations of power, this means reinvesting in current systems of stratification.

The "return to nature" in either Shepard or Bly is more than a separation from the mundane, from the effects of civilization; it is an exclusion of women. A gathering of men may have as its purpose making men more sensitive, by reconciling them with the image of their fathers—neither savage nor soft; but it is done by excluding women. Jake's decision to disappear in the wilderness is also a departure from homes inhabited by women. These actions reinforce gender differentiations, but with a twist. In the traditions of patriarchal discourse women are associated with nature, with the unreasoning and irrational, while men are perceived as beings capable of transcending material limitations and occupying the ethereal reaches of abstract thought and rationality. Jessica Benjamin cites Thomas Mann:

> The world of the day, of the sun, is the world of the mind. . . . It is a world of knowledge, liberty, will, principles and moral purpose, of the fierce opposition of reason to human frailty. . . . At least half of the human heart does not belong to this world, but to the other, to that of the night and lunar gods . . . not a world of the mind but of the soul, not a virile generative world, but a cherishing, maternal one, not a world of being and lucidity, but one in which the warmth of the womb nurtures the Unconscious. (Benjamin 1988, 147)

For men to "return" to nature for healing is, symbolically, to return to the "maternal one . . . the warmth of the womb." This movement away from the realm of the abstract to physical comfort is coherent with Bly's stated aim of healing men. But what is significant in this act is precisely the negation of women, the implication being that men can nurture men, reducing even the ancillary role prescribed for women in traditional definitions of gender. Instead of advancing a profeminist agenda, both the men's movement and *A Lie of the Mind* further marginalize women by increasing the distance—physical and metaphorical—between men and women, and by confining them to the "home," which has been deprived of its "maternal" function. Women are left with little choice. Either they fulfill the function of Maggie the Cat, as Beth does, or burn their homes and move to be with other women, as do Lorraine and Sally. They become handmaids serving the needs of injured men or are driven from view.

This is a very different image than that put forth by Haedicke and Bank. They locate within the contours of *A Lie of the Mind* very different spatial configurations. Haedicke envisions a transformation occurring within the cultural arena that carries the potential for empowering women, creating a truly democratic political space (1993, 91). Alternatively, Bank perceives a subversion of gender taking place in the fragmented representations of character and in the destabilized dialectic of self and other.

> Presence is always defined . . . in terms of absence: an absent person, a past time, a lost part of the self, a shattered dream, a jettisoned relationship, a place that is no place and every place. The search for and confrontation with the Other is inevitable and endless because it is the search for confrontation with the Self. (1989, 238)

Within this play of contradictions the issue of difference is raised only to be redefined in the discourse of the same. In both of these articles there is a call for a new spatial configuration based not on hierarchies of difference, but a politics that deconstructs the boundaries of marginality and opens a field of discourse in which positions of responsibility can be shared with pleasure.

However, the spatial relationships described by Haedicke and Bank are in direct opposition to those enacted by Shepard and Bly. The women focus on the potential for growth through intersubjective interactions across the boundaries of gender; the men reinforce differences by exacerbating the distances, seeking not to share space but to further limit the mobility of women. Significantly, all are seeking the means of securing their identity, the women by reducing the limits of their marginality; the men by intensifying those limits. The primary difference is that currently men are more likely to occupy the positions of authority needed to enact their desires.

The desire to enforce spatial relationships is not a trait peculiar to men, however. The construction of boundaries to secure an individual or collective identity seems to be a necessary, if not universal, activity.

Sue-Ellen Case recognizes the need to envision a protected space that
resists surveillance for lesbian interaction on the information highway.
"On the other side of the issue, when a specifically 'lesbian' address
does cross the lines, it requires a certain protection, when traveling
through generally accessible nets. For while Sappho's serene isle may
exist, it floats within a wide, sexist sea"—a sea occupied by "the anti-
homosexual Right agenda" that can bring to Sappho's isle "a kind of
invasive terrorism" (Case 1995b, 341). To protect the community that
affirms her identity, Case suggests that "a different kind of encrypting
the lesbian address might better serve as a security system" (341). The
difference between the urgency with which Case seeks to defend a lesbian discourse and with which the men's groups want to limit feminist
discourse is the question of authority. Case *seeks a safe space* in which to
avow her sexuality, while the men *resist attempts to limit* their ability to
express their masculinity. Outside of this significant difference the
effect is the same: to enforce the distances that secure identity.

   In a world of increasing fragmentation, security systems may be
necessary not only to avoid the terrorism of virulent prejudice but to
contain questions that threaten the integrity of the self. This double
movement to keep at a distance and to hold in is not only an individual
propensity but a cultural discourse as well. But such constructions
come at a cost.

> The separation of spheres intensifies as society is increasingly
> rationalized. As in erotic domination, the process replicates the
> breakdown in tension: the subject fears becoming like the object he
> controls, which no longer has the capacity to recognize him. As the
> principle of pure self-assertion comes to govern the public world
> of men, human agency is enslaved by the objects it produces,
> deprived of the personal authorship and recognizing re[s]ponse
> that are essential to subjectivity. On the other hand, private life,
> which preserves authorship and recognition, is isolated, deprived
> of social effectiveness. Thus societal rationalization negates what is
> truly "social" in social life. (Benjamin 1988, 185)

Benjamin believes the negation of the social is an effect of individualism, privatization, and consumerism. She links these precipitates of
capitalism to "long-standing dualisms in Western culture: rationality
and irrationality, subject and object, autonomy and dependency" (184).

Although Benjamin, too, falls prey to reinscribing binaries, specifically male versus female, she is cognizant that the problem has become systemic and is no longer merely the result of individual behaviors. "This means that male domination, like class domination, is no longer a function of personal power relationships (though these do exist), but something inherent in the social and cultural structures, independent of what individual men and women will" (186–87). To effect change, these binaries need to be deconstructed, allowing for the play of remainders rather than their conscription through spatial limitations. "As the practice of psychoanalysis reveals, breakdown and renewal are constant possibilities: the crucial issue is finding the point at which breakdown occurs and the point at which it is possible to recreate tension and restore the condition of recognition" (223). I suspect this will have, for feminists such as Sue-Ellen Case, an all-too-familiar ring to it. Who precisely is to yield ground in the process of breakdown and renewal? And how, precisely, are we to negotiate the recreation of tension and restoration of recognition?

Deeper structures that define a resistance to change need to be considered before these questions can be addressed. Talking allows us to negotiate immediate stresses and strains in intersubjective relations, facilitating responses to the breakdowns in which Benjamin invests a good deal of hope; hope that the boundaries can be attenuated in interactions between people. But these structures of difference are privileged factors and have become ingrained in our experience of subjectivity, where they limit our ability to recreate the tensions that allow for recognition. The resistance to acknowledging the experiences of others is, once again, not an individual decision, but is marked by the processes that define our relationship to the culture in which we live, a relationship defined not by a will to exclude but by the definitions of pleasure and their value to the structuring of identity.

NOTES

1. The musicality of the text is underscored by Shepard's recognition of the contribution made by the Red Clay Ramblers to the New York production. "But working intimately with these musicians, structuring bridges between scenes, underscoring certain monologues, and developing musical 'themes' to open and close the acts left me no doubt

that this play needs music. Live music. Music with an American backbone" (Shepard 1986, "Music Notes").

2. Control should not be mistaken for authority. Men continue to dominate this space—Frankie takes center stage on the couch, Baylor continually orders Meg and Beth around, and it is the home that Lorraine and Sally eventually burn to the ground as a means of ending the domination of the father. Rather than authority, women have responsibility for the home and its order.

3. Shepard acknowledges that in *A Lie of the Mind* he was attempting to use cinematic techniques in order to allow parallels between stories to be perceived (Rosen 1993, 2).

4. Shepard may have been drawing upon personal experience. Jessica Lange, to whom he is married, played Maggie in a revival of Williams's play. Other autobiographical coincidences occur in *A Lie of the Mind*, as well. See Schvey 1993, 14.

5. Feminism gave rise to concern about the feminine, but not women per se, at least in this perspective. Bly sees the effects of feminism as much less positive. "The strong or life-giving women who graduated from the sixties, so to speak, . . . played an important part in producing this life-preserving, but not life-giving, man" (Bly 1990, 3).

Chapter 4

Fantasy and Subjugation

The creation of boundaries through the articulation of space protects against the destabilization of subjectivity, while allowing the subject relative freedom of movement. The negative effect of these boundaries is that they place limits on others and on their ability to experience the same freedom of self-expression. These limits to subjectivity have powerful material consequences, as discourses on sex, race, and postcolonialism attest; nevertheless, they are primarily psychic structures—of indeterminate origin and conscious only when there is resistance. Once "performed," they are performative, defining limits on the accessibility of space, and as such become reiterable practices.

Boundaries are always negotiable, however, and demonstrate a degree of flexibility when encountering sufficient force. These negotiations seldom occur at the point of resistance because of their significance to the integrity of identity. They are typically deflected onto the materiality of the body, onto the planes of physical interaction or language, not to suggest that these are necessarily distinct. Where the definition of subjectivity is historical and reflects the accretions of time, talking—while in the service of this history and the limitations of the particular linguistic form—is a more immediate locus of negotiation. It is an opening onto intersubjective relations where issues of distance and limits can be discussed in relative safety, with greater potential for compromise, as we have seen with Begosian's *Talk Radio*.

In the discussion thus far, it is not clear what precisely is contained by these limits. This is, of course, ultimately an unanswerable question, but not one that can be ignored. The ability to negotiate and compromise, to mediate differences, implies at least a degree of fluidity, suggesting that, while not without structure, subjectivity is contingent upon circumstances and can be reformulated according to shifts in limitations. The influence of context on the form individuality takes indicates that whatever is contained by the definition of identity it is not self-generated. Instead it is an interactive process *uncontained* by the body, a process that includes communications with others, perceptions of the material world, and discursive/ideological practices. It is, in the conceptualizations of the postmodern, a continual circulation of intensities that resist the solidity of form. Indeed, the construction of identity can be seen as a response to this "boundlessness." Consciousness needs limits. It is virtually impossible to imagine space without end, for example—reason and emotion recoil from the thought of the limitless. The situation is similar to calls for the death of the subject. Reason can argue effectively for the nonexistence of the subject, but few can actually live such a life.

The structuring of the self, then, can be figured as an attempt to contain and direct the intensities of these circulations, to create patterns out of self-generated vectors of force and the contingencies emanating from outside the body. Identity, therefore, is not the articulation of an individual, but the location of an experiencing and expressing self in an existing range of possible communities that support patterns of behavior appropriate to the subject. The positive affects arising from the sense of security provided by limits (as freedom from the limitless) intensify the investment made in structures of subjectivity. This happy combination of control and expression makes us resistant to change.

According to this formulation, subjectivity is inherently conservative, not in the strict political sense—although the effects are certainly political—but as an ecology. We resist alterations to the environments in which we construct our way of life. This is a problem only when the concept of the individual becomes so paramount in dominant ideologies that injustices to others are tolerated—consciously or not—because we are content. This may explain, in part, why differences are intensified when pressures threaten the contexts in which we live.

The desire to maintain comfortable social environments is frequently perceived as an investment in social institutions. Citizens who adopt the values espoused by a society—both implicit and explicit—are expected to make sacrifices, including their lives, in order to perpetuate institutions. But the discourse of patriotism, a form it frequently takes, is seldom realized as an active support of an institution. Abstract concepts may serve to motivate individuals, but when push comes to shove, sacrifices are most frequently made because of investments in intersubjective relations.

> The identity of socialized individuals forms itself simultaneously in the medium of coming to an understanding with others in language and in the medium of coming to a life-historical and intra-subjective understanding with oneself. Individuality forms itself in relations of intersubjective acknowledgement and of intersubjectively mediated self-understanding. (Habermas 1992, 153)

It is in the interactions between subjects that the boundaries of identities are defined, reinforced, and reproduced. The nexus of individuality and ideology is not the immediate connection between the subject and what Althusser calls the ideological state apparatus (1971) but is a mediated process between the subject and other individuals who hold values similar to, or in opposition to, those espoused by the institution.

The introduction of the third term in the reproduction of ideology complicates the process of individuation. Subjectivity reflects identifications with a number of ideological positions, but intersubjective relationships, while perhaps privileging one system of values (religion, work, etc.), are a complex process of evaluating the compatibility of differing beliefs. The intensity and valence of the relationship is determined by the degree to which our values match. These determinations are ultimately unquantifiable and are "measured" not only as intensities of like and dislike but of indifference as well. There will always be a degree of ambivalence. Intersubjective relations can seldom be defined by a particular attitude toward another person because subjectivity is never simply defined by relations with others and institutions.

The definition of the body arises from experiences of pleasure and pain. These events result in the privileging of certain objects, narratives, and images and encourage individual efforts to institutionalize structures that give pleasure or avoid pain. Those with sufficient power will seek to guarantee their availability upon demand and will urge their incorporation into ideological systems of belief. Indeed, the protection and preservation of the means to pleasure becomes the *primary* obligation of those placed in positions of authority; and this has required, historically, the subjugation of certain portions of the population to the will of those in power. While this subjection is achieved initially by coercion, its perpetuation is accomplished through ideological interpellation and the administration of the spaces occupied by and in between those institutions. It is the institutionalization of a "will to pleasure" that underlies Foucault's introduction to *The History of Sexuality:* "What was formed was a political ordering of life, not through an enslavement of others, but through an affirmation of self" (Foucault 1980, 123). An affirmation whose expression is found in the experience of pleasure, but whose guarantee lies in the oppression of others.

The intersection of the pleasures of subjectivity, the perpetuation of social institutions and the intersubjective is the focus of Jean Genet's *The Balcony.*

Fantasy and The Balcony

Irma's Grand Balcony is a house of prostitution, though it may be called just as accurately a house of illusions. It consists of elaborate chambers, really theaters, in which clients enact a scenario by portraying a figure whose position has assumed archetypal proportions in society, such as the judge, bishop, general, and beggar. Donning elaborate, oversized costumes and *cothurni* the customers inhabit the image of a social functionary and enact a narrative that leads to their sexual gratification. Three elements seem necessary for a successful fantasy: the outlines of a persona through which the customer can reimagine himself, a mimetic action that parodies the function of the persona, and an object—usually the body of a woman—with which to express the force of the desire. If these elements are in place and the narrative precisely inflected in the playing out, the effusive pleasure of orgasm will be experienced.

But only if the structure is correctly articulated in every detail and the roles adhered to precisely will climax be achieved. The man assuming the role of Bishop insists that the sins he is forgiving are real—or at least that he *believe* they actually were committed. Similarly the Judge wants to be punishing real crimes; the General, his horse to have the correct attitude toward her rider; the Beggar, lice in his wig. These specifics, which define the context for the fantasy, must be convincing, or at least give the appearance of truth, for the narrative to commence. There is, in fact, an incredible inflexibility when it comes to the articulation of the image. If there is insufficient verisimilitude in the imaging of the persona to be inhabited, it will be impossible for the client to divest himself of the functions defined by his occupation outside of the Balcony. This is a necessary condition for investing in the sexual fantasy: he must believe he is other than he is. And to do this he must create a concrete, alternative identity through which he can experience the power of living a reality divorced from his ordinary existence.

Belief in the persona does not imply complete identification, however. There must always be one element that is recognizably false. "They all want everything to be as true as possible. . . . Minus something indefinable, so that it won't be true" (Genet 1966, 36). The inattention makes absolute proximity impossible because it continually reminds that the image is nothing more than a mask. To lose sight of that fact would make fantasy impossible because illusion depends on its immateriality or, in terms more relevant to Genet, the absence of function. To transgress the boundaries of simulation, at least in one direction, is to live the reality of the mask—to *become* the bishop, judge, general; to live their duties and responsibilities. This is, after all, the greatest fear in certain approaches to acting (however apocryphal), that I will lose sight of who I am, and my subjectivity will merge with that of the character I am playing. Fantasy depends on the image being empty, on the absence of function, on the knowledge that we are not the persona we inhabit. "He's my body, as it were, but set beside me" (Genet 1966, 53).

Once the appropriate structure is in place, the narrative interaction between the image in which the man has dressed himself and the prostitute on whom and through whom he will live his fantasy can commence. The structure, once embraced, is not forgotten, however, for at any time within the procession of events, a check may be made to ensure the defining elements of the image are rigidly in place. Interrupting the fantasy is less important than making sure the context is firmly established. On the other hand, the scenario, while clearly scripted, is open to permutation in ways the mise-en-scène is not.

THE GIRL: The procession has begun. . . . We're passing through the City. . . . We're going along the river. I'm sad. . . . The sky is overcast. The nation weeps for that splendid hero who died in battle. . . .

THE GENERAL: *(starting)* Dove!
THE GIRL: *(turning around in tears)* Sir?
THE GENERAL: Add that I died with my boots on! (Genet 1966, 27)

This rewriting of the script serves only one purpose, and that is to intensify the pleasure the man receives from living through his chosen image. The innovation has no inherent value but is significant because the thought of being buried with his boots on conforms to the contours of his desire on this occasion. In another session, he might well chastise her for inappropriately embroidering upon his fantasy. The narrative must be grounded in the image being portrayed, but the story serves the rhetorical function of propelling the client toward the moment of pleasure. If the momentum falters, a variation on the theme is necessary to immerse the client once again in the pursuit of rapture.

The third element necessary to bring the fantasy to a successful conclusion is the presence of another party, a body upon which or through which the fantasy can be realized. It is the prostitute, sometimes with the pimp, who enacts the story for the purpose of giving the client pleasure. None of the fantasies in *The Balcony* appear to lead to sexual intercourse; instead, satisfaction derives from the ability of the other actors to reflect back to the customer the image he wishes to "become." The Judge says,

> I'm pleased with you, Executioner! Masterly mountain of meat, hunk of beef that's set in motion at a word from me! (*He pretends to look at himself in the Executioner.*) Mirror that glorifies me! Image that I can touch, I love you. (18–19)

Love, in this instance, is the ability to see himself in the other as he wishes to be seen. But it is not the self-adoration of Narcissus who became enamored of his own reflection. Rather, the solipsism of the Balcony requires that the other performers adopt a persona through which the primary actor can see, not himself, but a merging of himself with the image. The "Judge" sees Arthur, who is playing the Executioner, as an executioner, because he can then see himself as a judge; similarly with the thief.

> My being a judge is an emanation of your being a thief. You need only refuse—but you'd better not!—need only refuse to be who

you are—what you are, therefore who you are—for me to cease to be . . . to vanish, evaporated. Burst. Volatilized. Denied. (19)

The supporting actors must assist in creating the environment and playing out the fantasy in order that the client may believe in the image they reflect back to him, may believe in the illusion to the brink of ecstasy.

Genet does not depict the ecstatic moment until the end of the play when Roger, inhabiting the image of the Chief of Police, castrates himself. While the full implications of this scene will be discussed later, it is significant that the experience of ultimate pleasure occurs with the character's back to the audience (93), because pleasure, like pain, is beyond representation. The rapture the Bishop receives from masturbation—"what have my hands been doing? . . . you make it possible for the most tender and luminous sweetness to ripen in warmth and darkness" (13)—happens only in description, with the act concealed under the vestments of office. Pleasure resists containment in language because it is liquid, like the seminal fluid of the Bishop, which will "flood the world" (13), or the blood of Roger, which saturates the carpets of the Balcony. Yet it lies at the heart of the experiences in Irma's studios; it is the molten core the client wants to experience.

In the rooms, a highly structured context is created, within which a more flexible and manipulable narrative is set in motion that will enable the man to experience the effusiveness of pleasure. Within the triadic structure of image, narrative, and object there is a necessary and yet contingent movement from solid structure to uncontainable liquidity: from the inflexibility defined by the image (often made manifest in the size and elaborateness of the costume) that resists variation, to the plasticity of the narrative that changes course according to the demands of desire, and finally to the dissolution into the fluid pleasure of fantasy inscribed on the body of another. But ecstasy resists containment in the body, as it does in language, where it is reduced to metaphor and description, which cannot bridge the gap between the constructions of representation and the inexpressible disseminations of *jouissance* throughout the body. The moment of ecstasy cannot be seen, only its effects.

Pleasure is always present, however. It manifests itself throughout the fantasy and not only in the moment of climax that may define its primary manifestation. Pleasure is experienced in the putting on of the costume—"Mitre, bishop's bonnet, when my eyes close for the last time, it is you that I shall see behind my eyelids, you, my beautiful gilded hat . . . you my handsome ornaments, copes, laces" (7); and in the unraveling of the narrative —"Madame! Madame, please, I beg of you. I'm willing to lick your shoes, but tell me you're a thief" (20). It is found in the rigidity of the context—"A general reprimanded by his horse! You'll have the bit, the bridle, the harness, the saddlegirth, and I, in boots and helmet, will whip and plunge!" (24); and in the fantasy itself that has brought him to the studios of the Grand Balcony, decorated to enhance the narratives of pleasure.

The clientele of the Grand Balcony base their fantasies on roles institutionalized within society. The narratives parody specific authorities by stripping them of their content and eroticizing the image. In the world of Genet, this is the moment of theater, in which the actor immerses himself in a character, that is, in the play of significations detached from the material operations that authorize the sign. In precisely this instant Plato locates his critique of representation and attempts to ban theater from the Republic. Mimesis destabilizes society through the privileging of unauthorized copies that subvert the integrity of the social fabric, that elevate image over "the real and the commonplace." For Genet, however, this use of the sign has salutary effects because it allows the habitué of the brothel to transcend the alienating effects of social conformity and experience a reunification of self in the solipsism of pleasure; but Genet is not optimistic.

Parody for the purposes of transcendence assumes, indeed requires, the existence of a functionary who enacts the obligations of a socially defined occupation, including the "job" of begging. Without a beggar there would be no image to be appropriated; therefore, at least for the purposes of fantasy, poverty is necessary for the ecstatic experience arising from this particular narrative. This is not to say that society is created for the purposes of fantasy; rather, once in existence, the structuring of society provides images that are eroticized so that the mundane can be transcended. Men come to the brothel to escape the "commonplace" of their lives, whether plumber or ambassador, through a theater that allows them to assume an identity absent in their material existence. They inhabit a role for the specific purpose of pleasure, but in making the choice they acknowledge the significance— even in their absence—of the functions and values attributed to that position and thereby accept as their own the ideologies that support the character they have appropriated. The Chief of Police wishes his image enacted in Irma's house of illusion because it will make his job easier, because "My name will act in my place" (53). Once his name is used in constructing a fantasy, it is granted a significance beyond that authorized by the state; it takes on a sanctity through those whose investment in the name commits them to the perpetuation of the position within society.

The preservation of a social structure does not require persistent vigilance, however, for within the discourse of ideology, images take on a force of their own. A mirroring relationship is established between the image exploited for the purposes of ecstasy and that linked to function; between them, the "image, like your name, reverberates to infinity" (Genet 1966, 92). Within the infinite regress of reciprocal reflection, the image is replicated so completely and frequently that the functionary can disappear, or be replaced, without damage to the signifier. The man playing the bishop can become the Bishop by wearing the appropriate costume in a public procession.

> No one could have recognized us. We were in the gold and glitter. They were blinded. It hit them in the eye. . . . Exhausted by the fighting, choked by the dust, the people stood waiting for the procession. The procession was all they saw. (72)

The image lives on regardless of the body; indeed, it carries more force because without the physical manifestation the inevitable contradictions between the signifier and the signified, between the person and their inevitable failure to satisfy the obligations implied in the image, are veiled.

The decision to assume the function of an image destroys the efficacy of the persona as a means to pleasure. When the three men who have been impersonating the bishop, judge, and general immerse themselves in the "real and commonplace," they abandon the ecstasies of the brothel.

> We're going to live in the light, but with all that that implies. We— magistrate, soldier, prelate—we're going to act in such a way as to impoverish our ornaments unceasingly! We're going to render them useful! (80)

Immersion in the real displaces the unauthentic element that allowed them to be constantly reminded that the story they were enacting was an illusion. By accepting the function associated with the costume they have rendered the image unsuitable for their own fantasies. When they return to the Balcony, they will need a new image, which for the Bishop will involve dancing naked in the simulation of a cathedral square.

> You spoke of dancing? You referred to that notorious afternoon when, stripped—or skinned, whichever word amuses you— stripped of our priestly ornaments, we had to dance naked on the cathedral square. I danced, I admit it, with people laughing at me, but at least I danced. Whereas now, if ever I have an itch for that kind of thing, I'll have to go on the sly to the Balcony, where there probably is a room prepared for prelates who like to be ballerinas for a few hours a week. (80)

The need for a fantasy to exist on a plane outside of function will keep Irma's house of illusions in operation and, in this instance, reinscribe the position of ballet within the ideology of culture. Maintaining social structures becomes a means of maintaining the sources of pleasure; while perpetuating sources of fantasy reinscribes the significance of social structures.

Herein lies the profound pessimism of Genet. The experience of pleasure as the by-product of the play of meanings between image and function calls into question our ability to alter social structures. Are we willing to sacrifice the sources of pleasure to endure the pain of change? Genet, as much as anyone, is aware of the authority of the image in our lives and explores, through the revolution occurring outside the walls of the Grand Balcony, our potential to affect the institutions in society that define the relations of power, reinforce ideologies of oppression, and administrate the spaces in which we live.

The motivating force that ignited the rebels in their attempt to overthrow the government has disappeared in the reduction of the revolution to a clash of two forces with opposing objectives: to save or destroy the state. The struggle between the war machines has been simplified to a question of good versus evil. "It's the combat of allegories. None of us know any longer why we revolted" (57). The reduction of the conflict to its lowest common denominator provides the rebels with a focus and defines their function while, at the same time, diminishing to insignificance the diversity of grievances that gave rise to the need to resist. The foundation upon which the revolution is based slips away, and, with the growing distance between the need for change and the desire to effect change, the movement loses sight of the material causes of the rebellion. The revolution, like the Balcony, "takes off, leaves the earth, sails in the sky" (37). As it ascends, function is left behind, and the search begins for an image that will fuel the flagging desire for change.

ROGER: If you want a woman to lead your men forward, then create one.
THE MAN: We looked for one, but there aren't any. We tried to build one up: nice voice, nice bosom, with the right kind of free and easy manner. But her eyes lacked fire, and you know that without fire . . . (56)

They locate the fire in Chantal, a prostitute from the Balcony who has left Irma and joined her lover Roger, a leader of the rebellion. "At first people were fighting against illustrious and illusory tyrants, then for freedom. Tomorrow they'll be ready to die for Chantal alone" (68).

The need to replace function with an image spells the end of the revolution; the rebels have left the commonplace and entered into fantasy.

IRMA: He belongs to the Andromeda network.
THE CHIEF OF POLICE: Andromeda? Splendid. The rebellion's riding high, it's moving out of this world. If it gives its sectors the names of constellations, it'll evaporate in no time and be metamorphosed into song. (51)

The accuracy of the police officer's prediction is realized when Chantal is asked to sing from the palace windows and encourage the forces to continue the struggle.

In becoming the figurehead, Chantal completes the triad of fantasy, providing the rebels with the opportunity to transcend the horrors of armed insurrection and find pleasure in reliving the narratives of 1789 and Delacroix's *Liberty Leading the People*. "In order to fight against an image Chantal has frozen into an image. The fight is no longer taking place in reality, but in the lists. Field azure" (58). The revolution becomes a conflict between competing images: the rebels promise the deferred pleasures of a new order, dressing them in the robes of romanticism; while Irma and the Envoy present the tatty garments of the brothel suffused with the aura of past pleasures and the guarantee of immediate gratification. Although the exact sequence of events is unclear, the results are not.

> The slowness of the carriage! We moved forward so slowly amidst the sweaty mob! Their roars were like threats, but they were only cheering. Someone could have hamstrung the horses, fired a shot, could have unhitched the traces and harnessed *us*, attached us to the shaft of the horses, could have drawn and quartered us or turned us into draught-horses. But no. Just flowers tossed from a window, and a people hailing its queen, who stood upright beneath her golden crown. (71)

Irma's fear that the rebels will be so carried away with passion that they will "leap, without realizing it . . . into reality" (50) proves groundless; instead, they pass into the realm of simulacra in search of the transcendence through pleasure. Instead of reordering the material world, the rebellion, upon seeing the procession of images that heralds the return of the old order, softens and then becomes fluid, "throwing kisses" (71).

The Balcony has come full circle. The structures of fantasy and the desire to experience pleasure that are played out in the studios of Irma's house of prostitution are reenacted on the barricades of the revolution. Through the layers of protection that conceal the peccadillos of those who act in the theaters of the Balcony, the rebels "can sniff the orgy behind the wall of flame and steel" (31), and they want it. Like Artaud's plague, the promise of rapture and the wish to experience the becoming-fluid of pleasure is contagious and permeates the institutions that define society and resistance to it. The rebels try to overturn the existing pantheon of simulacra, but in the process fall prey to illusions of the new and begin resuscitating images that have been lying dormant, rather than creating an alternative order. The revolution fails to articulate what Foucault calls a new episteme (an ordering of knowledge that breaks with existing habits of thought) and recycles, instead, already discredited paradigms of pleasure.

Roger recognizes this failure when he returns to the Balcony not to repeat the fantasy that led to his relationship with Chantal but in search of a new image through which he can express his disillusionment at the collapse of the rebellion. "And outside, in what you call life, everything has crashed. No truth was possible" (93). He chooses to emulate the nemesis of the uprising, the Chief of Police, a narrative that finds resolution in self-castration. Roger, in portraying the man credited with destroying the revolution, enacts his impotence: his inability to plant the seeds of a new world order. Ironically, his choice also deifies a new representation that strengthens and perpetuates the existing state organization and the system of ideologies on which it is founded. By embodying the policeman, Roger allows the Chief of Police to withdraw, leaving a simulacrum to stand in his place; or, in the words of Carmen, "you're dead, or rather . . . you don't stop dying and . . . your image, like your name, reverberates to infinity" (92). The person fulfilling the function of Chief of Police is no longer important because, within the echoes of Roger's self-mutilation, an image is formed and defined: "as soon as I feel I'm being multiplied ad infinitum, then . . . then ceasing to be hard, I'll go and rot in people's minds" (84). He can cease to be hard because the simulacrum has become rigid and, through his rotting in people's minds, the office will transcend the "mud of the commonplace," becoming an unquestioned authority, an image of supreme ideological force. "Though my image be castrated in every brothel in the world, I remain intact. Intact, gentlemen" (94). The narrative may lead to pleasure through self-mutilation, but those who embrace the erectness of the form will value the office of Chief of Police because through its image they will experience the theater of pleasure: ecstatic transcendence through fantasy.

The revolution begins again at the end of *The Balcony*, as it must, because it offers for those involved the material for creating a crucible of fantasy. This does not mean that Genet thought rebellions inevitably fail, though that is certainly the pessimism of the play; rather, revolutions crumble because of the dependence on simulacra, because of an investment in images grounded in the existing order of things. To overthrow a system is to abandon the theaters of pleasure and to embrace function for the sake of the function, which is not the same thing as renouncing ecstasy. Rather, it is a question of relocating pleasure outside the boundaries of fantasy, in relationships that do not depend on the triad of image, narrative, and object. Irma seeks it with Carmen in the "wonderful figures that we'll spend the nights together calligraphing" (40). Roger found it, fleetingly, in his relationship with Chantal. "I love you *with* your body, *with* your hair, your bosom, your belly, your guts, your fluids, your smells" (55; emphasis added). Their love appears to be reciprocal.

CHANTAL: I love you because you're tender and sweet, you the hardest and sternest of men. And your sweetness and tenderness are such that they make you as light as a shred of tulle, subtle as a flake of mist, airy as a caprice. Your thick muscles, your arms, your thighs, your hands, are more unreal than the melting of day into night. You envelop me and I contain you.
ROGER: Chantal, I love you because you're hard and stern, you the tenderest and sweetest of women. And your sweetness and tenderness are such that they make you as stern as a lesson, hard as hunger, inflexible as a block of ice. Your breasts, your skin, your hair are more real than the certainty of noon. You envelop me and I contain you. (58–59)

But their love is impossible because for Chantal he is an illusion, a "melting," and not the material reality she is for him, and because the allure of transcendent rapture is too great a temptation for her. "I plunge into the adventure, and I escape you" (55). In her escape, she returns to the world of the Balcony from which Roger sought to rescue her; she once again becomes an object in a narrative that will inspire men to fulfill the image of revolution. She will not be enveloped, she will not contain; she will become an image.

Within the immobility of that image, linked to a narrative and an object, the rebels can become fluid. The assumption of a mask and costume allows the man to experience the power of the character he is playing within the context of the fantasy; similarly, mounting the barricades introduces the workers and the peasants to the excitement of living out an insurrection by assuming the role of the revolutionary. When the ecstasy of release is over, they resume their lives, investing once again in the images they sought to overthrow. "Their roars were like threats, but were only cheering" (71). The return to an established order is a contradictory experience. On the one hand, they recognize their failure in the face of the simulacra, while, on the other, they can see in that construction the possibility of a return to rapture. "Their awakening must be brutal. No sooner is it finished than it starts all over again" (35). The recognition that the mask is an illusion throws into sharp relief the distance between the image and the actor, between the experience of rapture and the alienation of function. The intuition of power through ecstasy creates both a thirst for more and a recognition of impotence. This doubling, the fact that I am not the mask that gives me pleasure, endows the image with greater authority—at least in my eyes—and increases my determination to preserve the structures that support the simulacra.

What they seek through transcendence is the force of a coherent self—the experience of the body prior to representation, before the divisions necessary if language is to define it. They desire a subjectivity that has been lost in the specularity of Lacan's mirror, where the image of the self far exceeds the ability to fulfill it; in the ideology of Althusser, where the self is surrendered in the interpellation by institutions that promulgate systems of belief; but perhaps most of all in Adorno's administrations of the state, where they lose themselves in the divisions and subdivisions of society according to the obligations of mundane function. It is their dream to overcome these alienations that "tore [them] brutally from that delicious, untroubled state" (Genet 1966, 79–80). They seek this fluid, undividable self in the studios of the Balcony.

But there are other costs exacted by the desire to experience pleasure; debits inscribed on the bodies of the other who make fantasies possible. The Grand Balcony cannot dissolve; it is a business based on profitability, an institution with responsibilities to its clients. The studios are the crucibles in which the alchemical transformation of dross into gold, of image into the fluidity of pleasure, can take place. The women provide the environment in which the elements of fantasy—image, narrative, and object—can lead to the moment of rapture. The walls of the studios, the windows covered with padded draperies shield the interaction of client and prostitute from contamination: from eyes that would see through the veil of illusion and from voices that would remind the customer of his worldly function—he is not a leper about to be miraculously cured by a vision of the Immaculate Conception of Lourdes, but a banker (Genet 1966, 32). The architectural and decorative structures hide the masquerade, the self-adoration before mirrors, the becoming an image, the playing out of the narrative, the experience of dissolution in the moment of consummation. The studios are opaque, impervious to the metamorphoses that occur. The women who work in this house of illusions are similarly constrained, because it is in the space defined by Irma and the prostitutes that fantasy can take place. One provides the mise-en-scène; the others enact the scenarios: the criminal judged by the magistrate, the horse mourning the death of her general, the penitent seeking absolution from the bishop. It is in a society of women that the illusions can be created; through women offering up their bodies so that the heterosexual man can immerse himself in an image, for the sole purpose of experiencing the narcissism of pleasure—the disappearance of the woman, of the studio, of the balcony, of his wife and family—the absence of responsibility. For these transfigurations to occur the prostitutes must commit themselves to the demands and desires of the clients. They need to maintain a certain objectivity that denies them the opportunity to inflect the action with the terms of their desires; and should they slip, they are chastised for the violation of *his* fantasy.

The discipline required by their job exacts a price from the women. Their opportunity to experience pleasure is limited to the scenarios; they are forced to find pleasure in male narratives.

CARMEN: My blue veil, my blue robe, my blue apron, my blue eyes. . . .
IRMA: They're hazel.
CARMEN: They were blue that day. For him I was Heaven in person
    descending on his brow. I was a Madonna to whom a Spaniard
    might have prayed and sworn an oath. He hymned me, fusing me
    with his beloved colour. (38)

The adoration of the bank clerk provides her with rapture, but rapture based on his pleasure, on his need for her to be immaculate so that he can ejaculate. Outside of the mise-en-scène, Madame Irma demands that they refrain from talking about their experiences, providing them with no means for contextualizing the feelings generated during the sessions. Instead, her employees are allowed to play cards and await the arrival of the next client who needs their services.

The greatest cost, however, lies in the distance that exists between life in the brothel and the world outside. For Carmen, being a prostitute means separation from her daughter. "Everything inside me now yearns for my daughter" (32). Irma sees Carmen's longing to go to "the nursery in the country" (30) as a complex illusion. To leave the brothel is exceedingly dangerous; "there's fire and water, rebellion and bullets" (31), and were she to survive the journey, her daughter would receive her not as a loving mother, but as "the fairy godmother who comes to see her with toys and perfumes. She pictures you in Heaven" (31). Her advice to Carmen is to sublimate the desire to see her daughter in the garden.

IRMA: Your daughter is dead . . .
CARMEN: Madame!
IRMA: Whether dead or alive, you daughter is dead. Think of the
    charming grave, adorned with daisies and artificial wreaths, at
    the far end of the garden . . . and that garden in your heart,
    where you'll be able to look after it. . . .
CARMEN: I'd have loved to see her again. . . .
IRMA: You'll keep her image in the image of the garden and garden
    in your heart under the flaming robe of Saint Theresa. (40)

She extols her to transform the yearning into a fantasy and to use the figure of her daughter as her clients use their fantasies, as "an imperceptible light in the imperceptible window of an imperceptible castle that they can enlarge instantly whenever they feel like going there to relax" (34). Turning her daughter into an illusion could serve a pleasurable function, whereas the current situation only causes pain. But Carmen will have to pay the price by severing herself from the material pleasures in seeing and touching her child. She must limit herself to serve him.

Women's desire is a virtual absence in *The Balcony*. Like Carmen, Irma is unable to inhabit the image that would give her greatest pleasure; she cannot be a lover. Instead her desire is circumscribed by male sexuality.

It was you who forced him on me. You insisted on there being a man here—against my better judgment—in a domain that should have remained virgin. . . . You fool, don't laugh. Virgin, that is, sterile. But you wanted a pillar, a shaft, a phallus present—an upright bulk. . . . You stupidly forced him on me because you felt yourself ageing. (53)

While women frame male fantasies, guaranteeing the possibility of pleasure, men penetrate the world of women, limiting their ability to express their needs. The one instance in which Irma does reveal her

desire is with another woman. "You're not only the purest jewel of all
my girls, you're the one on whom I bestow all my tenderness" (39). The
intimations of lesbian desire are never made manifest, however, but
remain cloaked in metaphor. "I'll teach you figures! The wonderful figures that we'll spend the nights together calligraphing" (40). As if this
potential were perceived and feared, the two women are never alone
together onstage after this scene, and they are soon separated by the
intrusion of Arthur, the "upright bulk" the Chief of Police has insisted
on positioning in the domain of women. Granting agency to female
desire poses a threat to the dialectic between image and function
because it necessitates questioning the validity of the images and the
authority granted to the institutions on which men depend for structuring their fantasies.

Fantasy and the MLA

As perceived by Jean Genet in *The Balcony*, (male) heterosexuality
defines its pleasures in the discourse of fantasy. However, the parameters of this discourse are found not only in the excesses of the brothel,
but in the organization of space (both public and private), in the definition of representations, the authority to appropriate an image, and in
the narratives of power that offer an object through which to experience
pleasurable release. The implication is that the relationship between
fantasy and reality is reciprocal—the experience of the quotidian is
replicated and reinscribed by the images of fantasy; and the structures
of fantasy are authorized by the practical administration of everyday
life. This is not to say the two are interchangeable, far from it. One
depends on function, on the release of demand through the recognition
of commitment and responsibility; while the other finds expression in
the solipsism of narratives that locate pleasure in the negation of function. Our experiences of the everyday and fantasy, nevertheless, have a
common ground: the need to find channels that give definition to
desire and permit the expenditure of demand.

The relationship between men and feminism can serve as an example. Men's ambivalent relationship to feminism is defined, at least in
part, by the play between fantasy and function: in the contradictory
images that position women as the object of male fantasies; in the
dialectic between those ideologies that affirm the value of change and

those that maintain the status quo; and in the conflicting desires to preserve authority while removing structures that constrain women from
experiencing themselves. Opposition to equal rights for women arises
from the anxiety produced by the disruptions necessary for change.
The loss of the object alters the narratives of pleasure and threatens the
images of masculinity adopted by men to negate the mundane realities
of their lives. The immensity of the problem, the depth of the ideological construction of gender, becomes apparent in the contradictions with
which men are confronted when they attempt to align themselves with
feminism.

That women resist this attempt is not surprising because it is male
discourse that has made the mobilization of women necessary and
because, in the last instance, feminism is not about men or the relationship between the sexes but what it means to be a woman and the interactions between women. This is not a simple project, but one that is
confronted by recurring difficulties—internal, as women attempt to
reconcile the diversity of sexualities, racial and ethnic origins, and cultural identities; and external, as they face conservative men who wish
to maintain existing definitions of difference and relations of authority,
and face liberal men who ally themselves with feminist discourses.
Therefore, it should not be surprising that women have little patience
with men's problems and are profoundly suspicious of men who claim
to be feminists. They understandably dread, should men be positioned
within feminism, that women, like Chantal, will be subjected to the
same processes of objectification they seek to escape, that their attempts
to free themselves from patriarchy will be subverted by a diversionary
discourse that insists upon perceiving feminism through the problematic of male subjectivity.

Alice Jardine, Judith Mayne, Elizabeth Weed, and Peggy Kamuf
confronted this problem when they served as respondents to papers by
Stephen Heath, Paul Smith, and Andrew Ross at the Modern Language
Association (MLA) panel on "Men in Feminism." The panel was
divided into two sessions. In the first, the men presented papers that
defined their relationship to feminism; at the second, the women
responded. This form raises issues central to understanding the problem of men in feminism: "two sessions organized by a man, with
women once again responding, reacting—as always in the negative
position. . . . What if the men had responded to the women?" (Jardine
1987, 54). What *if* the women had spoken first?

The person speaking first is given the opportunity to construct the parameters in which all future discourse is to take place. The men created a context and defined the terms, positioning themselves within a landscape that is conducive to their interests. The respondents had to locate themselves in relation to the mise-en-scène established in the first three papers. The one site the women could not occupy is that of subject. This configuration is predicated in the title of the panel that places "men" as subject and "feminism" as the object of the preposition; and reinforced in the essays of Heath, Smith, and Ross, who argue, from very different perspectives, the position of *men* in relation to feminism. Other options were available, such as the perhaps more provocative possibility of talking about feminism in men or as Jardine puts it, "men as feminists" (Jardine 1987, 54). Stephen Heath compounded the problematic by circulating to the participants an essay on the subject of men and feminism prior to and in addition to the paper presented at the convention, thereby positioning the discourse and the participants in relation to the topic well in advance of the conference. Placed second by the male organizer, the women had to either accept the limits defined or attempt to dislodge the initial construct and replace it with an alternative; thus Jardine's reference to the negative position.

Situated in the position of respondent, Jardine, Weed, Mayne, and Kamuf feel obligated to acknowledge the papers presented in the first session and, to a greater or lesser degree, demonstrate an appreciation of the men's concern for the issues of feminism. Referencing the earlier papers, if only as an act of etiquette, reestablishes the context and valorizes the men as the subject. The women, thus positioned, proceed, with whatever grace or acerbity, to point up the difficulties of men locating themselves in relation to feminism and to underscore the problems and contradictions within the papers presented at the first session. They can never, however, speak out of context, create their own mise-en-scène without positioning themselves in opposition, as other.

Having set the stage, the men define images for themselves and articulate "narratives that possess a point-of-view (unified or otherwise) and that unfold (problematically or not) across a field of binary oppositions" (Mayne 1987, 63). Andrew Ross, in "Demonstrating Sexual Difference," approaches the question of men in relation to feminism obliquely through a discussion of Sutcliffe, the Yorkshire Ripper, a serial killer who pleaded diminished responsibility because he believed he was carrying out a moral mission to rid the world of prostitutes. Ross's "intention is to help reveal the incriminating silence of an entire social logic bound over to the necessity of predicating men and women as fixed social categories" (Ross 1987a, 53). His paper goes beyond an attack on tendencies to universalize, however, and claims that men must be perceived individually and their acceptability to feminists determined case by case. In this paper, the image he inhabits is that of an objective observer who depends upon the discourse of the law; but in an essay written for the book, *Men in Feminism,* the question of objectivity becomes a mute point because Ross believes his feminist training has already placed him within feminism. In "No Question of Silence," Ross differentiates theoretical men from biological men in response to Alice Jardine's breakdown of men in feminism into "the Silent Majority [opposed to feminism], the Divide and Conquerors [appear to support but fail to in practice], and the Allies" (Ross 1987b, 86); and he then subdivides the theoretical allies according to age.

> It is more plausible to expect, say, an *older* male feminist to occupy all three of Jardine's categories at different times or at the same time in different contexts (this is not intended as an ageist slur on older male feminists; I am referring to men whose personal intellectual history includes a substantial pre-feminist phase), than it is to expect him to occupy only one. (Ross 1987b, 86–87)

He exempts himself from the older group and identifies himself with younger theorists:

> for whom the *facticity* of feminism, for the most part, goes without saying; in other words, there are men who are young enough for feminism to have been a primary component of their intellectual formation (I offer my own as an example: the politics of feminism came first, democratic socialism later). (Ross 1987b, 86)

The structure he is creating is that of a family, positioning himself as the son with feminism as the mother, and conflating older male theorists with democratic socialism as the father. For Ross his position in feminist discourse is not open to question because he was weaned on feminism before the intercession of the father (democratic socialism). This Oedipal construct allows him to imagine himself outside the ideology of patriarchy; a move supported by his insistence on differentiating

theory from the body. In the world Ross constructs, the subject as theo-
rist can be isolated from the inscriptions of gender on the socialized
body. It is not my intent to use the trope of the family to describe the
pleasure Ross takes in feminism (though for some I have done just that)
but to define the image he occupies in order that he can be other than
he is.

Paul Smith and Stephen Heath perceive the binary of men and
feminism as a difference that needs to be negotiated, though their
approaches are quite different. Smith does follow Ross in differentiating theoretical feminism from practical applications by limiting the discussion to the academy, and further by asserting that "women's studies
has been relatively well integrated into the institutional and discipli-
nary structures of the academy" and by focusing on feminist theory "as
the bearer of whatever further political promise feminism offers in the
academy" (Smith 1987, 33). Having privileged feminist theory, he then
undercuts its radical potential claiming it is one of several discourses,
"in many ways not easily separable from the general 'theory' that has
worked its way into studies in the humanities over the last ten or
twenty years" (33). Elevating feminist theory to the level of general theory may or may not be condescending, but by ignoring the ways in
which it *is* easily separable from other theoretical discourses he reterri-
torializes feminism not so that it includes but is *included in* the field of
study in which he engages. By simultaneously limiting and delimiting
feminist discourse, Smith defines a position from which he can engage
feminism.

Smith does not locate himself "within" feminism in the same way
that Ross does; rather, he situates himself on the boundaries, in the
margins as a beneficial irritation who will perturb thought and keep it
from ossifying. "In the context of academic feminist theory these men
might perhaps do something akin to what women do within theory
more generally: that is, they can be there to help to subvert, unsettle
and undermine the (seemingly rather fast to settle) laws of the discourse" (Smith 1987, 39). The metaphor of the grain of sand that may
yet prove to be a pearl shortly gives way to a more subversive policing
function.

Indeed, from the point of their impossible—provocative, offensive,
troublesome—position in or near feminism, [men] might be able to

> help keep in view the referent which most of our current theory is
> all to eager to defer. (39)

The desire to play the provocateur gives way under the weight of the
double infinitive "to help" and "to keep," revealing the image of the
good cop who takes "an interrogative, but sympathetic role" (39). The
interrogation has the purpose of maintaining (the) law and (dis)order,
thereby legitimating the presence of men in the discourse of feminism.

Stephen Heath resists positioning himself within feminism and
argues eloquently the impossibility and undesirability of men trans-
gressing the boundary. He is cognizant, in ways Ross and Smith are
not, of the ideological inscription of patriarchy on his conception of
himself as subject, and the prejudices that interpellation brings to bear
on his relationship to feminist discourse. There is no assumption in his
paper that theory is in some way divorced from his experience as a
male in everyday life. Instead, Heath struggles to define a distance that
will allow him to create a positive and noninterfering relationship with
feminism. He arrives, ultimately, at "something like Irigaray's admiration" (Heath 1987a, 30).

Heath is cognizant of the problems of the position of admirer.

> The word, yes, is old-fashioned, is tangled up with ideas of love
> and courtship (the heroine's "admirer's" in this or that classic
> novel), is eminently deconstructible as the original senses are
> teased out and we find the notion of considering with astonish-
> ment and stupefaction moving into that of contemplating with
> reverence and esteem and gratified pleasure. (Heath 1987a, 29)

However, he locates in Luce Irigaray's recuperation of the word in *An
Ethics of Sexual Difference* a basis for defining his position. Admiration,
for Irigaray and Heath, is "the 'sudden surprise' of the new and the different that precedes objectification of the other as this or that quality,
this or that characteristic" (Heath 1987a, 29). Irigaray claims it offers

> [w]hat has never existed between the sexes. Admiration keeping
> the two sexes unsubstitutable in the fact of their difference. Main-
> taining a free and engaging space between them, a possibility of
> separation and alliance. (Heath 1987a, 29)

Heath acknowledges the utopian dimensions of the concept but nevertheless sees it as a position from which he can ask: "how do I change,
who am I if I listen and respond to feminism, if I understand with its
understanding?" (Heath 1987b, 44). There is something admirable
about this argument, and I will return to it in the last chapter, but there
is also something disconcerting.

The image Heath defines for himself is that of the student who
learns from feminism, which is a necessary relationship, but one that is
not unproblematic. The difficulty with the teacher-student relationship
is that the burden of proof can be too easily shifted onto the authority
figure: "that [feminism] must change me beyond any position to fall
back on, beyond any foregone security" (1987b, 45); "what is at stake in
men's coming to terms with that fact of recognition, understanding,
determination for change, with the whole process of women changing
things for themselves and for us" (1987a, 31). Resisting the responsibility of changing men, Alice Jardine responds that "we don't even want
your admiration (even if it's nice to get once in a while). What we want,
I would even say what we need, is your work. . . . *You still have everything to say about your sexuality*" (Jardine 1987, 60). Although Heath
states repeatedly the need to work, he neither outlines a project nor
suggests how one is to go about that work.

Peggy Kamuf locates another problem in Heath's appropriation of
Irigaray's admiration. She quotes Irigaray at greater length to make
two significant points. First, admiration arises when "the first
encounter with some object surprises us, and we judge it to be new or
very different from what we have known up to then or from what we
might have supposed it to be" (Kamuf 1987, 83). Admiration is a passion that occurs when we are taken unaware and when we judge it to
be novel in terms of our previous experience. To maintain the position
Heath is describing would demand of feminism "perpetual newness,
perhaps the lawless rule of the monstrous" (83). Second, in Irigaray's
definition, admiration "has no identified contrary, it does not, in other
words, already depend on a binary or dual repetition" (83). Heath's
definition, however, is based on a preexisting binary: the male subject
and feminism. To avoid this snare Heath is forced to "locate 'admiration' on a more or less imaginary map" (84). Heath cannot be an
admirer, in the sense Irigaray uses the term, because he has already
defined a binary position—his relation to feminism. To insist upon the

term would mean obliterating the boundary he has been careful to maintain: "the autonomy of feminism" (Heath 1987a, 31).

These ambiguities shift the perspective on Heath's positioning of himself in relationship to feminism. On the one hand he recognizes difference and wishes to maintain the integrity of both his own subjectivity and the feminist project. At the same time he insists that men, as least in theory, are already in feminism, "which has to include men, their transformation, in its project" (1987a, 31). Heath wants to maintain a distance but fears the "irreducibility" of women's experience and men's "will quickly become not difference and contradiction but a gulf, as though between two species" (31). A proximity is sought that positions him outside of feminism but that promises communion at some horizon. Similarly, Heath recognizes the need for men to change but, in assuming the position of an admirer, displaces the need for men to work onto women, who must continually surprise and offer what is new, if the passion of admiration is to be maintained. Out of these contradictions a new image begins to emerge. The student is replaced with (or defined as) a man who, in expectation of pleasures deferred to the moment of their coming together, watches women reveal themselves.

Stephen Heath, Paul Smith, and Andrew Ross conjure images that define how they wish to be perceived by feminists. With *the very best of intentions*, they colonize positions that offer them the promise of pleasure. They achieve this by articulating a context that limits discourse to the subject of men against a landscape of feminism. Within this articulation images arise that contradict, at the same time they complement, the stated objective of investigating the points of intersection between men and feminist discourses. For Ross it is that of a petulant son; for Smith, the provocateur; for Heath, the voyeur. In each instance, there proceeds from these personae a narrative of transgression. Smith claims authority to enter into feminist discourse as he deems appropriate; Ross presumes penetration of the boundary has already occurred and that it is a question of getting used to his presence; Heath focuses his gaze across the boundaries of difference and awaits the surprising revelation that will activate his admiration. These violations of the body of feminist theory hold out the promise of pleasures that are not purely academic. Rather the academy, like the studios of the Balcony, becomes the specific site for the repetition of fantasies that permeate social intercourse at all levels.

What differentiates the MLA panel from the relationships established in *The Balcony* is that the women respondents do not accede to the narratives created by the men. Their refusal to accept men into the folds of feminism disrupts the semiotics of pleasure denying them the opportunity to "become fluid," requiring, instead, that they remain in or retreat from the positions they have articulated. This does not mean there is no pleasure for the men, but that it must lie elsewhere.

Beneath the narratives constructed through the papers, another source of pleasure is being exploited. The men realize they will meet with resistance, thereby creating a dynamics of power. This, ultimately, is the significance of the organization of the panels. Assuming the positions of authority, a structure is created based on divisions and the threat of transgression—men *in* feminism. The format locates women in opposition, setting in motion the narrative of power that guarantees pleasure, either in the form of conflict or in the joy of victory, should the women simply accept their arguments. The respondents are in a no-win situation as soon as they agree to participate, because at that point the narrative is initiated and the women are positioned in a male discourse. The locus of authority and the wielder of force are two images that underscore the structures of male domination and underwrite the guarantees of pleasure in a patriarchal society. The narrative played out at the MLA, as the women well understood ("with women once again responding, reacting"), was a reinscription of male authority. It is a form based on the very real threat of sexual violence, of men in feminism, not only in the discourses of theory or in the excesses of fantasy, but in the hierarchies of everyday life.

The effects of male subjectivity on the lives of others cannot be reduced to men's investment in the narratives of fantasy. Nor are the attendant desires to maintain the structures of oppression that support the images used to create the illusion that we are other than we are sufficient, though they do provide a degree of complexity. As we have seen in the plays of Begosian, Shepard, and Genet, the discontents of masculinity are linked to other sources of pleasure, primarily determined by the definition of communities of inclusion and exclusion. The point I wish to make here is that men use patriarchal authority to contain the "other" in order to experience the pleasures of their sexuality.

The danger of this analysis is that it portrays women, once again, as mere victims of men's aggression. This is a disservice to both the women and men involved. The fact is that feminism has achieved a degree of institutional legitimacy particularly within the academy, despite the continuing disparity in the distribution of resources and the backlash of gender conservatives. There is, therefore, a certain amount of authority already invested in the women who participate in the panel. Indeed, it could be argued that, if only within the discourse of feminism, they represent the majority position. While it could be argued that there is a certain ludic quality to the event, an inverse of the carnivalesque where those in positions of "real" authority adopt the role of plaintiffs, there is a juridical force in the position of respondent that challenges patriarchal hierarchies and validates feminism as a discourse of power. Moreover, the panel allowed for a reinscription of the boundaries of feminism by disputing the men's claims to be "in" feminism. The respondents, tactfully and with relative grace, maintained the differences between genders while indicating an agenda for men to pursue that would support the trajectory of feminism and define what they believe to be appropriate positions for men to inhabit. It would be ludicrous to say that there is no pleasure in this project or that it did not, in very real ways, valorize the subjective positions of the women (participating and watching) or allow them to exercise agency in the face of patriarchal authority.

Exchanges across divisions of difference are Gordian knots and cannot be reduced to moralities of good and bad. The dynamics of pleasure, where it is sought and in what form it is achieved, resist the clear attribution of intent. Rather, they need to be seen as complex negotiations over the control and release of intensities—never simple. This relationship is complicated by the fact, despite numerous discourses to the contrary, that we are all subjects. Granted, there are numerous contexts in which the subjectivity of a person is denied expression or even existence, where their ability to exercise agency is severely limited if not absolutely refuted; but this does not mean that people are incapable of acting subjectively. We all create boundaries of difference, define for ourselves communities of identity, negotiate access to positions of authority, fantasize and desire to maintain the structures that provide us with pleasure. This does not mean we are all equal or even that we are equally, on some essential level, subjects. What it means is that we all establish relations with institutions, facilitate interactions with others, and locate means for expressing the intensities of our existence. Activities that are not done in isolation, but in a dynamic that is an intertwining of intersubjective relations and the uses of pleasure.

Chapter 5

Toward a Theory of Subjectivity

Any theory of subjectivity is built, ultimately, on metaphors, a foundation less substantial than shifting sands. To seek an ontology of being, as Artaud tried to do in his desire to rid himself of his bourgeois body, to get to something essential, is to be faced with a vast and unending silence—a silence as complete as death, were it not for the intuition of something experienced, "an insistent and inexhaustible demand" (Butler 1993, 90), a quiet recognizable only when punctuated by thought, by language—that which makes metaphor possible.

The necessary relationship between language and consciousness both gives us the tools to question our existence and creates a screen that makes answering these questions impossible. The systems of representation and differentiation that allow us to identify ourselves as subjects also obscure from understanding the field of investigation. Three men of the theater, all of them French, who have in very different ways undertaken the existential "quest" for understanding the grounds of subjectivity have at least one thing in common: the need for abjection. For Artaud, the search followed a trail illuminated by drugs and the desire to know experience outside of a language that stole his breath from him and negated his existence in the inevitable twists of objectification. "In pursuit of a manifestation which would not be an expression but a pure creation of life, which would not fall far from the body then to decline into a sign or a work, an object, Artaud attempted to destroy a history" (Derrida 1978, 175). The history he attempted to destroy was that inscribed on his body, that which kept him from knowing the ecstatic joy or agony of a "pure creation of life":

> to resolve by conjunctions unimaginably strange to our waking minds, to resolve or even annihilate every conflict produced by the antagonism of matter and mind, idea and form, concrete and abstract, and to dissolve all appearances into one unique expression which must have been the equivalent of spiritualized gold. (Artaud 1958, 52)

Only "after a meticulous and unremitting pulverization of every insufficiently matured form" would it be possible "at the incandescent edges of the future" to retain his breath and in that containment *experience* the "rarity" of his being (51).

Genet also abjected his body, but to destroy a different kind of history. Through crime and homosexuality, he sought to put himself beyond the prescriptions of social order, creating for himself a hierarchy of criminality, the "true" criminal being the one with nothing to lose, who through his actions isolates himself from the controlling force of society. "After taking the big leap into the void, after cutting myself off from human beings as I've done, you still expect me to respect your rules? I'm stronger than you and I can do as I like" (Genet 1966, 146). The culmination of his persistent attempts to negate the social was not the desire to create life, but the recognition that, like Lefranc in *Deathwatch*, he could not get beyond the social—there was always something to lose. Genet found himself perpetually trapped in a multiplicity of representations and realized that outside of these reflections there was no certainty, only an infinite regress of mirrored images.

> He who gets it will be there—dead—for eternity. The world will centre about it. About it will rotate the planets and the suns. From a secret point of the same room will run a road that will lead, after many and many a complication, to another room where mirrors will reflect to infinity. . . . I say infinity. . . . the image of a dead man. (Genet 1966, 69)

The images reproduced in the parlors of Irma's Grand Balcony offer only surfaces embodied by nameless figures about whom nothing is known. "You know the refrain? The Queen attains her reality when she withdraws, absents herself, or dies" (Genet 1966, 85). Like the throngs who throw carnations rather than bombs at the false dignitaries parading through the streets, the performatives are read with scant attention paid to the performances that bring them into being, the performances that disappear with barely a trace. "Performance's only life is in the present. Performance cannot be saved, recorded, documented, or otherwise participate in the circulation of representations *of* representations: once it does so, it becomes something other than performance" (Phelan 1993, 146). Similarly with subjectivity. Once introduced into the "circulation of representations *of* representations," it is only what it appears to be—which is, for Genet, synonymous with death. But to be outside the system of reflections is to say with great precision and an anguish we can only begin to imagine: "I really am all alone!" (Genet 1966, 163).

Samuel Beckett takes a different path altogether. His is an intellectual rigor that seeks through the continual distillation of thought to identify the minimal precipitates of consciousness necessary to locate the subject. Molloy, at the end of Beckett's novel, returns to his bourgeois home in such an abject state that the person and the context in which we first encountered him are no longer compatible. The semiotics through which the character is defined is seen, in the end, as a ruse concealing the impossibility of locating existence, because, if only in afterthought, we see with clarity that Molloy, in his final abject state, remains defined by the context, the system of significations that articulate reality. We understand at the end of *Act without Words I,* as the fetal figure stares at his hands, seeing nothing but his own body, his own inability to construct or end a life, that we have not yet reached a point sufficiently fine to say what subjectivity is. Nor in the pauses of *Breath,* that brief signature of a life—from birth to death in a landscape of detritus, an inhalation and an exhalation framed by the scream of a woman "in vagitus"—do we hear what we are, other than an absence.

The profound pessimism attending the negative ideal of abjectness underscores the impossibility of breaking through the layers of Heideggerian facticity that encrust our existence and render impossible a knowledge of being.

> Lying behind each eye that sees, there exists a more tenuous one, an eye so discreet and yet so agile that its all-powerful glance can be said to eat away at the flesh of its white globe; behind this par-

ticular eye, there exists another and, then, still others, each pro-
gressively more subtle until we arrive at an eye whose entire substance is nothing but the transparency of its vision. This inner
movement is finally resolved in a nonmaterial center where the
intangible forms of truth are created and combined, in this heart of
things which is the sovereign subject. (Foucault 1977, 45)

The contradictions—a nonmaterial center, intangible forms—that subvert Foucault's description of the ontological quest for the subject
underscore its impossibility. The existential dilemma in the conceptualization of the nonbeing of subjectivity marks the angst of the high-modernist project, and the postpessimism implicit in the postmodern death
of the subject, a negation of a negativity. But in between, or perhaps to
the side of pessimism and nonpessimism lies another possibility, one
articulated by Herbert Blau.

As for what happens in the theater, there is a point in every work
when you have to ask through the work itself: How much of what
you want to believe can you justify, given the world that is being
reflected upon? *Is it necessary for this act to take place?* . . . it is what
brings the music of the will of meaning into performance. (Blau
1982b, 197)

Between subjectivity and the performative lies the performance, the
doing. And to deny subjectivity or insist only on the circulation of surfaces reduces the act of performing to the inconsequential at best, to
nonsense at worst.

But action does seem necessary if only when, in the stream of solipsism, the self is no longer reflected back to itself; and despite the fact
that in the construction of the macropolitical, acting may appear to be
meaningless in the face of institutionalized mechanisms of oppression.
If doing, if performance is integral to the construction of self and culture, then a model of subjectivity is needed that can account for the
ways in which we act and are acted upon.

To do so, it is necessary to shift from the sexualities of Genet to the
intellectualities of Beckett, specifically in *Not I.* This play is here
brought into conversation with two other texts that present distinctly
different conceptualizations of the body: Freud's modernist theory of
the instincts and their effects on the definition of the subject; and the

body without organs, a trope for discussing the intensities of presence, in the phantasmaphysics of Deleuze and Guattari. The fourth "text" is a model developed in neural biology describing the transmission of energy across synapses. The intent is not to privilege one discourse over another but to expand the repertoire of metaphors available for the description of subjective processes. Such a theory is necessary if we are to understand the dynamic relationship between the body and the practices that define subjectivity, particularly those that are central to erecting and maintaining the boundaries of difference.

The surreal image described by Beckett in the stage directions to *Not I*—an elevated and faintly lit mouth and the lower, shrouded Auditor—is sufficient to support the claim that the play is located in an interior, a psychic landscape of the mind. The fragmentary, disembodied mouth and the occluded, desexualized body of the listener resist even being perceived as human beings, virtually proclaiming a metaphysics of alienation. A seemingly untransgressable distance separates the two figures, who attempt to communicate with each other through language and gestures, in the pauses, but who are unable to make contact. They cannot reach across the darkness that defines their existential isolation. A sufficiently desolate picture when conceptualized as the inability of individuals to communicate, it gains in force when conceived as a metaphor for an intrapersonal dynamic.

Beckett's vision of the subject, within this static staging, is an image of despair. The hopelessness implicit in this construction of the "I" is the effect of an ordering that creates in spatial terms a hierarchy of privilege. Dominant is the mouth, the speaking subject that, in its faltering, streaming insistence, tells of the woman and her catastrophic situation. The Auditor, the obscured hearing subject, can only receive the verbal onslaught and respond weakly with "a gesture of helpless compassion" (Beckett 1984, 215). This vertical relationship within an otherwise horizontal stage composition defines a simple modernist model of decentered subjectivity—that is, I seek myself in the imaginary distance between what I say and what I hear myself say.

It is not, however, a matter of splitting the distance between selves, of geometrically bisecting a line constructed between two points. For the question of subjectivity, even within the modernist framework, is not one of symmetry, but of asymmetries. The authority of the mouth as the locus of the self, where the sound of the voice is proof of existence, is continually disrupted by the intrusions of other voices. Who, for instance, interrupts the flow of words issuing from the mouth? Who challenges the integrity of the voice, forcing the Mouth to insist upon the difference between itself and the "she" of whom it speaks: "what? . . . who? . . . no! . . . she!" (Beckett 1984, 217)? Is it the same voice, the same "I" that demands that the Mouth consider all of the possibilities? "she" did not know . . . what position she was in . . . whether standing . . . or sitting . . . but the brain— . . . what? . . . kneeling? . . . yes . . . whether standing . . . or sitting . . . or kneeling . . . but the brain— . . . what? . . ." (Beckett 1984, 217). Is it the same "I" that laughs at the thought of a merciful God, or screams at the thought of help? And who is "she"? Is she, as seems likely, both the one who speaks and who is spoken of? the self conceptualized as other? simultaneously the "I" and the "not I"? The interruptions, on the one hand, and the description of "she," on the other, make the simple conception of a split subject—the Mouth who speaks and the Ear who listens—untenable. Beckett has effectively undermined the apparent significance of his own powerful stage image.

Disrupting the dualist concept of subjectivity does not eliminate the question of the subject, however. In naming the play *Not I*, Beckett insists on the existence of the "I"; he does not negate it. The personal pronoun functions in the linguistic semiotic as a shifter: an empty signifier that can be appropriated by any number of signifieds. It can be used by all conscious subjects with equal authority. But every use of the shifter, every assertion of the "I," also denies all previous claims by insisting on the difference between myself and all others who claim to be subjects, thereby simultaneously defining the "not I." This does not mean that every claim to subjectivity is ultimately meaningless. Each articulation of the self constellates particular contents that for that moment signify the "I," establishing boundaries to what is meant by the self.

In fact, the indeterminacy of the pronoun does not lessen its signifying force; rather it enhances its power. Each content brought into relation with the dominant signifier becomes a sign in its own right, even if it only signifies "not I." The effect is an interrelated field of signs arranged around the "I," or in the formulations of Deleuze and Guattari, a spiraling chain moving away from the signifier (1987, 113). And, while the potential for leaping to any point on the chain exists, the potential for infinite extension is not paralleled by a similar drift toward the center. "The jumps are not made at random, they are not without rules. Not only are they regulated, but some are prohibited: Do not overstep the outermost circle, do not approach the innermost circle" (Deleuze and Guattari 1987, 113). The limits on our ability to "know" ourselves, the boundaries that differentiate us from others and that separate consciousness and unconsciousness, keep us from the loss of identity and from enacting the "essential drama" of Artaud, "the revelation, the bringing forth, the exteriorization of a depth of latent cruelty by means of which all the perverse possibilities of the mind . . . are localized" (Artaud 1958, 30). The authority of the dominant signifier and the contents associated with it are sufficient to define the subject as different without succumbing to the desire to know the preconscious self.

Therefore, although I cannot *know* myself, I can gather together signs that allow me to assert my subjectivity under the auspices of the "I." This sleight of hand does not limit my self-understanding; instead it provides an environment for the seemingly infinite proliferation of self-knowledge, thereby enhancing the force of the dominant signifier.

> [T]he signifying regime is not simply faced with the task of organizing into circles signs emitted from every direction; it must constantly assure the expansion of the circles of spiral, it must provide the center with more signifiers to overcome the entropy inherent in the system and to make new circles blossom or replenish the old. (Deleuze and Guattari 1987, 114)

Therefore, the "I" with which I nominate myself is not only a symbol for the network of signs implicated in my experience but for the unexpressed force, the *signifiance,* that "collects" the signs and links them to the dominant signifier. This excess, which permits me to identify myself, nevertheless resists objectification, providing me only with the intuition of a presence beyond self-knowledge. Ironically, my inability to represent that force to myself, and my desire to know it, leads to an ever-increasing proliferation of the signs used to define subjectivity. As my ability to encompass the full range of representations deteriorates, my conception of myself begins to fragment into discrete but interrelated images of identity that will alter depending on the circumstances of any particular moment. My inability to articulate a unified concept of myself through the proliferation of signs indicates the relativity of who I am. Far from a stable term through which I can know myself, the

"I" provides a momentary illusion of self that will be transformed as the signs are substituted, one for other. I become father, son, teacher; and as I specify myself in relation to these functions—good or bad, active or passive—I recognize the impossibility of a coherent identity and sense my nonexistence in ever-fragmenting articulations of subjectivity. But caught in the vertigo of despair, I realize I am only disappearing in words, in a *semiotic* of subjectivity. There is still the body that attests to my existence.

Within the context of the body, the Mouth and the Auditor (the ear) deserve no special privilege. The plane of signification may describe a hierarchy in which signs of the greatest intensity appear to occupy positions nearest to the dominant sign; but within the fluctuating intensities of the body such determinations do not exist. Instead there are forces, an "energetics of presence" that accounts for jumps between signs, the creation of new signs, and the entropy of others, which are not accounted for in semiotics but which must be in any theory of subjectivity. Not because these forces describe an origin—such ontological considerations are irrelevant; it is sufficient that they are there—"Nothing but bands of intensity, potentials, thresholds, and gradients" (Deleuze and Guattari 1983, 19). So when the Auditor raises its arms, I am not seeing an empty signifier, but an effect of subjective processes that operate beyond the veil of signification. The material mouth of the actor dimly lit upon the stage acknowledges a deeper, unrepresented corporeality: the reality of a body expunged of metaphysics, defining the vehicle that exists prior to, and that makes possible, thought.

Identifying the body in Beckett's work is made difficult by the seemingly conscious effort to erase it from consideration at every conceivable opportunity. The fragmentary mouth and the shrouded figure are the obvious examples, but more significant is "she," the other described in the Mouth's narrative. Walking through a field in April, picking cowslips, she has a catastrophic experience. Her return to consciousness is partial; she is effectively paralyzed, unable to sense her physicality, "she did not know . . . what position she was in . . . imagine . . . what position she was in! . . . whether standing . . . or sitting . . . but the brain" (Beckett 1984, 216). The continually functioning brain and the absence of physical sensations appear to place limits on the field of investigation, but the body refuses exclusion. Ironically, the mind must affirm the existence of the body—consider all the possible positions, standing, sitting, kneeling, lying—in order to reaffirm the dominance of thought. The insistence of the physical, its precedence over consciousness, its necessity as the vehicle of thought, make it central to defining the material reality of Beckett's vision. The corporeal—debased, reduced to its most fundamental contradictions—allows Beckett to conceive of the body as the indeterminate center of two polar oppositions: one temporal, one spatial.

The onset of the catastrophe that leaves the "she" of *Not I* in a state of paralysis is preceded by a description of her movements, which seem, initially to be an ominous forewarning of what is about to occur, "a few steps then stop . . . stare into space . . . then on . . . a few more . . . stop and stare again . . . so on . . . drifting around . . . when suddenly . . . gradually . . . all went out" (Beckett 1984, 216). These phrases evoke the signals sent by the body to announce the onset of disruption, the footfalls of her impending death. But this reading is disputed when her life is described in exactly the same terms, "walking all her days . . . day after day . . . a few steps then stop . . . stare into space . . . then on . . . a few more . . . stop and stare again . . . so on . . . drifting around . . . day after day" (220). Life becomes a metaphor for death, and death for life. They are commensurate, and Bob Dylan's lyric, "Those not busy being born are busy dying," must be rewritten: "Those busy being born are busy dying."

Nor can solace be found in the cyclical vacillations between the inhalation and exhalation of *Breath*, another of Beckett's plays, through which one imagines a mythical moment of transfer from life to death. The optimism of life and the pessimism of death create a false dichotomy: the life of the body is the death of the body. It is a continuum, an uninterruptable movement that appears segmentable only in the stolen breath of thought.

> If difference, within its phenomenon, is the sign of theft or of the purloined breath [*souffle*], it is primarily, if not in itself, the total dispossession which constitutes me as the deprivation of myself, the elusion of my existence; and this makes difference the simultaneous theft of both my body and my mind: my flesh. If my speech is not my breath [*souffle*], if my letter is not my speech, this is so because my spirit was already no longer my body, my body no longer my gestures, my gestures no longer my life. (Derrida 1978, 179)

What she can know is neither her life nor her death; they are stolen from her in the moment of separation, spirited away onto the plane of representations. It is not the integrity of her body but her experience of it that is corrupted in the definition of being.

Her state of paralysis not only denies her awareness of physical posture but also negates emotional states, "as she suddenly realized . . . gradually realized . . . she was not suffering . . . imagine! . . . no suffering! . . . indeed could not remember . . . off-hand . . . when she had suffered less" (Beckett 1984, 217). The fact that I am asked to imagine the absence of suffering indicates that for Beckett it is a generalized state of being. Or it at least predominates over the alternative: "just as the odd time . . . in her life . . . when clearly intended to be having pleasure . . . she was in fact . . . having none . . . not the slightest" (217). The concepts of pleasure and suffering are used to describe two distinctly opposite physical sensations. They do not describe a continuum, however, in which the absence of pleasure indicates a plenitude of suffering, or vice versa. Rather, they are different responses to particular excitations that play across the body, that are not necessary to life, but inevitable consequences of it.

The body is, in the last instance, a corporeality subject to excitations that are interpreted as pleasure or suffering.

> We believe, that is to say, that the course of those events is invariably set in motion by an unpleasurable tension, and that it takes a direction such that its final outcome coincides with a lowering of that tension—that is, with an avoidance of unpleasure or a production of pleasure. (Freud 1953–74, 18:7)

As Freud implies, not all tensions are necessarily unpleasurable. It is the interpretation of the increases and decreases of excitation that define pleasure and suffering, "but the brain still . . . still sufficiently . . . oh very much so! . . . at this stage . . . in control . . . under control" (Beckett 1984, 218). This is not to deny the function of the body in conveying shifting intensities or in influencing interpretation, since the sensitivity of the perceptual system to excitations plays an informational role in the interpretative process. Rather, it is to claim that the body relays information in terms of magnitudes, and that the mind translates them into qualities. To understand this movement, I must shift focus from the speaking Mouth to the spoken of "she"—or more accurately, her sonorities. In the course of describing her catastrophic experience the Mouth alludes to three distinct sonorities: the speaking voice, the streaming, and the buzzing. It is in the irreversible movement between them that I can glimpse the outlines of a pragmatic theory of the subject.

She knows she is alive when she regains consciousness because of the buzzing. "found herself in the dark . . . and if not exactly . . . insentient . . . insentient . . . for she could still hear the buzzing . . . so-called . . . in the ears" (Beckett 1984, 217). The continuation of life is signaled; and the vibrations, Beckett's mental sentience, may affect the ears, but its undefined, uncertain, unimportant origins are within the mind. "in the ears . . . though of course actually . . . not in the ears at all . . . in the skull . . . dull roar in the skull" (218). The paradoxical description—it is a buzzing, a dull roar—underlines its indefinability and insists upon its metaphorical status. Neither she nor the Mouth know what it is, but they recognize its insistence. "what? . . . the buzzing? . . . yes . . . all silent but for the buzzing . . . so called" (218). The relentless buzzing represents the boundary beyond which lies absolute silence, the limit that begins from before birth and finds closure only in death. It connotes the energetics of the body, the determining factor of presence: what Deleuze and Guattari call the body without organs.

> The body without organs is an egg: it is crisscrossed with axes and thresholds, with latitudes and longitudes and geodesic lines, traversed by *gradients* marking the transitions and the becomings, the destinations of the subject developing along these particular vectors. Nothing here is representative . . . any more than a predestined zone in the egg resembles the organ that it is going to be stimulated to produce within itself. (1983, 19)

This is what Freud identifies as the instinct: "An instinct . . . never operates as a force giving a *momentary* impact but always as a *constant* one. Moreover, since it impinges not from without but from within the organism, no flight can avail against it. A better term for an instinctual stimulus is a 'need'" (Freud 1953–74, 14:118–19).

While it is possible to define the force within the body as an instinct or a need, it is impossible to give it a specific name until it finds expression through the body. A need defines an internal state that moves outward in search of "satisfaction, which can only be obtained by removing the state of stimulation" (Freud 1953–74, 14:122). The only means of naming an instinct, therefore, is through the identification of the object through which energy can be released. But a particular object does not necessarily correspond to a particular need, because the creation of a cathexis between demand and the other is subject to variations: the "object . . . is what is most variable about an instinct and is not originally connected with it, but becomes assigned to it only in consequence of being peculiarly fitted to make satisfaction possible" (14:122). The naming of an instinct, including Freud's cautious demarcation of the ego and sexual drives (14:124), is *a posteriori;* it occurs within the field of representations where it will be defined according to the values of the particular language. In fact, "instinct," "need" and "demand" can serve as examples, because they mark the culmination of a movement of energy from the undifferentiated field of force to the surface of language, where they are perceived as *concepts.* It is in the ordering process that an unknowable quantity (force) is differentiated into a quality (the instinct). The drives in Freud have more in common with the buzzing, so-called, of Beckett than with discrete functions, such as the survival instinct.

Knowledge of an instinct is possible only when the object cathected is identified and, through an act of deconstruction, the need hypothesized. In *Not I,* the differentiating activity occurs within the remaining two sonorizations. The smooth surface of the buzzing, disrupted only by the cyclical movements of the sound waves, the gradients of shifting intensities, is different from the sonority of streaming. The image of streaming implies limits, banks, and a bed and lacks the multidimensional timelessness of presence. It is inflected and bears the traces of language. "words were coming . . . a voice she did not recognize . . . at first . . . so long since it had sounded . . . then finally had to admit . . . could be none other . . . than her own . . . certain vowel sounds . . . she had never heard . . . elsewhere" (Beckett 1984, 219). Her voice, but not a language she understands. "mouth on fire . . . stream of words . . . in her ear . . . practically in her ear . . . not catching the half . . . not the quarter . . . no idea what she's saying . . . imagine! . . . no idea what she's saying! . . . and can't stop" (220). She has become possessed by these unfamiliar sounds, the biblical tongues of fire, the syntax of spirit. She hears only vowels, sounds created by the vibrated and distorted but otherwise unrestricted column of air that is her breath. But it lacks the rhythmic pattern of inhalation and exhalation; it is the aspiration of a voice that is unceasing and uncontrollable. "now can't stop . . . imagine! . . . can't stop the stream . . . and the whole brain begging . . . something begging in the brain . . . begging the mouth to stop . . . pause a moment . . . if only for a moment . . . and no response" (220). This unceasing, incomprehensible voice, the implacable voice within us, is not the syntax of speech but the current of desire: "a new polyvocality that is the code of desire" (Deleuze and Guattari 1983, 40). Desire: the channeled and incomprehensible force that speaks but cannot be understood.

Freud, as I read him through Derrida, uses the metaphor of breaching, the movement of energy across synapses, to describe the translation of the energy of presence into desire. "Breaching, the tracing of a trail, opens up a conducting path. Which presupposes a certain violence and a certain resistance to effraction" (Derrida 1978, 200). The definition of a pathway, a riverbed, gives direction to the instinct, but does not remove "the state of stimulation at the source." One breaching is never enough; there is always repetition—the repeated movement of intensities that mark the channel as useful as a means of release—and in that retracing is the origin of a memory. An effraction never results in complete satisfaction; there is always an excess that proclaims the persistence of the instinct, its continued production, and defines the differences between breaches:

> there is no pure breaching without difference. Trace as memory is not a pure breaching that might be reappropriated at any time as simple presence; it is rather the ungraspable and invisible difference between breaches. We thus already know that psychic life is neither the transparency of meaning nor the opacity of force but the difference within the exertion of forces. (Derrida 1978, 201)

But the pathways utilized by the instincts direct force through the body, no longer as undifferentiated force but as chains of intensities, as pulses streaming through the body. The canalization of demand, the creation of a vector of force, defines a motivation determined by the territories of the body affected by the pathway. Each link in the chain, each pulse is a sign, whose significance is determined by the quantity of force and the direction(s) in which it moves. Nor is the motivation necessarily singular—the need for food may manifest itself as sexual desire as well as hunger. The meaning carried by the sign is actually a promise, a promise that an object can be found on which the force can be expressed. The effraction of a particular path does not, however, lead to a specific "other," but merely promises a context in which that need can be satisfied, however incompletely. Nor does the teleological aspect guarantee that a suitable object will be found. Rather, the pathway that has been facilitated admits, by *exclusion,* a range of potential modes of expression. A neuron connects with other neurons that culminate and can induce movement in certain regions of the body. Until a particular response is activated, each possible movement remains only a potential.

The movement of force through the body is not a simple narrative line in which a demand seeks expression at one among a number of possible sites. Instincts are not univocal. Numerous effractions, of unequal force but related to the same need, occur simultaneously along a number of pathways; and the conduits exploited may motivate contradictory responses within the organism. Moreover, effractions of more than one instinct will occur at the same time, similarly utilizing a variety of openings, at differing magnitudes, and with the same potential for self-contradiction. The concept of a linear transference of energy through the body needs to be replaced with an image of multiple streamings from a variety of sources flowing together, each moving toward expression at a number of possible locations. The convergence of vectors is not necessarily compatible and may create flows based on affinities or resistances, tensions or facilitations. Moreover, not all of the resulting dynamic networks carry the same force; they can contradict each other. The disparity in relative strength will privilege certain needs, facilitating certain modes of expression, while those of lesser force may be denied access to certain forms of release and be required to locate other avenues of expression less conducive to the satisfaction of demand—indeed, in ways that may be detrimental to the body.

The force of the instinct is no longer an amorphous energetics, but an element in the stream of fluctuating intensities that define desire. It is the unrelenting pressure, of unknowable origin, that refuses to be silenced and yet is so frustratingly incomprehensible.

no idea what she's saying . . . imagine! . . . no idea what she's saying! . . . and can't stop . . . no stopping it . . . can't stop the stream . . . and the whole brain begging . . . something in the brain . . . begging the mouth to stop . . . pause a moment . . . if only for a moment . . . and no response . . . as if it hadn't heard. (Beckett 1984, 220)

The mouth of desire cannot be responsive to the demands of the brain—the whole brain or something in it—because the mouth is not an ear. Similarly, the movement of energy within the body cannot be stopped; it will find expression, somewhere. The difficulty, the impossibility is knowing precisely what gradient or gradients are being expressed.

There are, nevertheless, moments when it seems possible to know the destination of an intensity, to understand the syntax of desire. "straining to hear . . . the odd word . . . make some sense of it" (Beckett 1984, 221). She believes that in that word lies the meaning of her struggle: "something that would tell . . . how it was . . . how she— . . . what? . . . had been? . . . yes . . . something that would tell how it had been . . . how she has lived . . . lived on and on" (221). But to achieve that end she must hear the stream and glean from it its signification. "so intent one is . . . on what one is saying . . . the whole being . . . hanging on its words" (219). But she cannot know "something she didn't know herself . . . wouldn't know if she heard" (221). She cannot know because it is in the wrong language—the glyphics of intensities rather than the codes of language. This re-presentation of the originary energetics, in "edited" form, defines for Derrida a "primary" writing that

> cannot be read in terms of any code. It works, no doubt, with a mass of elements which have been codified in the course of an individual or collective history. But in its operations, lexicon, and syntax a purely idiomatic residue is irreducible and is made to bear the burden of interpretation in the communication between unconsciousnesses. (Derrida 1978, 209)

The idiomatic codification is likened by Derrida, through Warburton and Freud, to hieroglyphs, "pictographic, ideogrammatic, and phonetic elements" (Derrida 1978, 209). This image is principally spatial, however, and in being static loses the fluid dynamic of shifting forces. She cannot hear the word because the repetition that should make clear what she thinks she is hearing refuses to remain constant. The sign shifts with each pulse, as the intensities fluctuate so the meaning is transformed. On the brink of understanding, she cannot, but must wait until the flow of desire finds expression on the plane of representation.

What she can understand, her speaking voice, the third sonority, is heard only three times. When she speaks it is the result of a struggle to organize a coherent statement that will express the turmoil and uncertainty she is experiencing. "or grabbing at straw . . . the brain . . . there . . . on to the next . . . bad as the voice . . . worse . . . as little sense . . . all that together . . . can't [. . .] can't go on . . . God is love" (Beckett 1984, 221). The three-word phrase, "God is love," is insufficient to the task; it lacks adequate correspondence to the internal movement she is experiencing, "what she was trying . . . what to try . . . no matter . . . keep on [. . .] hit on it in the end . . . then back . . . God is love . . . tender mercies . . . new every morning" (223). Three words are expanded to three phrases, which in some labyrinthine way summarize for her the force of her existence—at least insofar as language is able to articulate that force in speech.

In the movement into language desire undergoes a process of translation from the fluctuating intensities, which describe the hieroglyph as a condensed flow of undefined contents, into the spaced linearity of language. The streaming sets in motion the cognitive functions of representation that, through a series of effractions, respond to the diversity of inputs by activating word/images that approximate, but ultimately fail to communicate the full force of desire. There is nonetheless a release and a temporary reduction in neural impulses. In the writing of Beckett, this temporary reduction in the force of desire is marked as the failure of language by the appearance of the ellipses. "God is love . . . tender mercies . . . new every morning . . ." The inability of language to accommodate the plenitude and the continually shifting intensities of desire drives language as the difference between force and release. The disrupted flow of language indicates momentary caesuras in pressure, ultimately acknowledging the failure of the body to expend itself: "all silent but for the buzzing."

This failure is also evident in the subsidiary modes of expression that lack the force to be represented but that, nevertheless, find expression through the activities of the body. The syntax of language is accompanied by effractions that lack the authority of the word but that find expression through pathways compatible with linguistic representations. They surround the word and encase its phonology, defining what Roland Barthes calls the grain of the voice. Once linked to the word, they trace differences in the evaluation of the representation that challenge the integrity of the signifier and the signified appropriated by it. They call into question and critique the system of facilitations and resistances that finds inadequate resolution in a particular word, a particular syntax. They define a minority, a force of desire that is not given a voice: "Never in truth represented or representable, though this is not to say that they have no effect upon the present scenography" (Irigaray 1985, 138). These effractions are experienced in the margins of consciousness and call into question the narratives used in many theories of the subject. They challenge images of universality and assumptions of closure; at the same time they are the marks of difference that point to alternative pleasures, and therefore give voice to the possibility of change.

Subjectivity, as imagined through the metaphor of the three sonorities in Beckett's *Not I,* resists concretization because it is inscribed within a dynamics of fluctuating intensities. Nevertheless, the outlines of a theory of the subject are perceivable in the movements that define the pathway to expression. For Deleuze and Guattari the movement of force from the undifferentiated energy of demand through the canals of desire to expenditure describes the interactions of three machines:

> every machine functions as a break in the flow in relation to the machine to which it is connected, but at the same time is also a flow itself, or the production of a flow, in relation to the machine connected to it. (1983, 36)

The flow of demand is disrupted in the canalization of desire, which shapes the flow that finds expression in the syntaxes of representation. This procession of energy is not a simple linear trajectory, as Deleuze and Guattari well understand. Instead, it is a complex process of intersecting vectors that combine and divide as they move through the body toward expression. "These indifferent signs follow no plan, they function at all levels and enter into any and every sort of connection; each one speaks its own language, and establishes syntheses with others that are quite direct along transverse vectors, whereas the vectors between the basic elements that constitute them are quite indirect" (Deleuze and Guattari 1983, 38). My subjectivity is defined by these movements, not in a particular locus of being, but in the fluctuations, convergences, resistances, and ultimate release of, or failure to release, energy.

But knowledge of the self, her knowledge of herself, lies not in these processes; understanding is determined by the forms of representation that are available for the construction of an identity. The metaphors of subjectivity do not describe a reality knowingly experienced, but they are tools for understanding the effects of my existence on the body. They allow for the conceptualization of certain structures that explain how the writings of Beckett, Freud, and Deleuze and Guattari intersect with neurological constructs to define a model of the processes of subjectivity. But this theory does not make me "available" to myself; rather, it positions me within the very systems of representation that define my distance from myself, that make it impossible for me to know myself. It is this distance that needs to be explored if this theory of subjectivity is to be complete.

In the analysis of realistic plays it is a commonplace that characters are to be understood "not by what they say but what they do." There is within this adage a warning that people in plays can be deceptive, that there are layers of action based around the concept of a public mask, the image presented to others, and the private persona, the character's self-image. The links between these two modes of interaction define the realm of subtext, where the reader is to locate an understanding of the characters' intentions. These objectives identify the play of desire within the characters, define their wants and needs. It is through the measure of the distance between public facade and private intent that "character," as a judgment, reveals itself. The assumption is that there are limits to deception, beyond which lies the "truth." While we are now sufficiently skeptical and question whether or not the truth of personality can ever be revealed, we nevertheless base relationships on the belief that we can predict how a particular person will respond in certain circumstances. And we are dismayed (or overjoyed) to discover how wrong (or right) we were in our assessment. However, actors also know they cannot judge the actions of characters. Negative objectives cannot be played with energy and commitment; an actor's responsibility is to find a positive motivation for the choices made by the character. The assumption underlying this second principle of acting is that regardless of the distance between what is said and what is done, characters believe they are behaving appropriately.

These two tenets define opposing positions. The first insists on the necessity of evaluating choices, while the second is equally insistent upon the inappropriateness of such judgments. Any expenditure of the body's energy is positive in that it allows for a reduction of excess force—within the energetics of demand there is no morality; and yet there are certain circumstances where release is resisted, and the body must locate an alternative means of expressing desire regardless of the potential for self-contradiction. It is at this point that the psychoanalytic terms displacement, sublimation, and condensation become useful and the idea of repression is constituted as descriptive of the socialized body; but they do not satisfactorily account for the discrepancy between what we say we believe and the contradictory ways in which we behave without "intending" to be deceitful. A theory of subjectivity must account for "lies of the mind."

Prior to the articulation of the body through the internalization of social practices there are few obstacles to the expenditure of energy. Any *innate* resistances to the expression of desire function by gross generalization. They define neither a motive nor an object but resist paths that disrupt the security of the preconscious being. Within the economy of the body, this does not mean that modes of release are undifferentiated. The binaries of tension and relaxation, pleasure and pain, and satisfaction and dissatisfaction define a field in which experience is measured in terms of attraction and repulsion, and in quantities rather than qualities. Any father who is left for any extended period of time with an infant for the first time has probably experienced the intensity of the child's distress when the mother leaves. It is usually only after the experience that we learn the baby was not rejecting us but missing the smell of the mother—a change in the infant's world that induces anxiety. A stable state is disrupted, and tensions at the change in circumstances are expressed as displeasure. This does not mean that there is an ideal homeostasis for the child located at some imaginary point of intersection of the three binaries just described. There is no center, just different positions within the field: "*attraction and repulsion* produce intense *nervous states* that fill up the body without organs to varying degrees . . . they designate, first of all, a band of intensity, a zone of intensity on [the] body without organs" (Deleuze and Guattari 1983, 19). More complex evaluations of intensities, that is, the introduction of qualitative differences to a system of quantities, and modes of reducing them in relation to alterations in the external environment, are not merely the result of changes in internal states, but the effect of interactions between the body and its environment.

As the infant's experiences with the father increase the degree of anxiety decreases (under most circumstances), permitting the father to become an object through which the child can experience a satisfactory release of energy. Initially the image of the father lacks specificity for the child; for instance, if the father has a moustache the infant will respond positively to any man who has one, and negatively to any one who does not. Gradually the baby is able to identify a greater number of features that relate specifically to the father, allowing the child to discriminate between different qualities. This process of differentiation allows the child to recognize a particular object of desire according to an increasingly sophisticated taxonomy. It also means, however, that the force of desire within the body will not be expressed until *the* object of desire is present, or a suitable alternative—someone with sufficiently similar characteristics to allow for cathexis.

The definition of an object of desire is not determined only by exposure and the delineation of particular characteristics. Any expression of energy is going to be met with a return that will valorize the mode of expression (the warmth of a father's embrace) or not (the turning away of a stranger). Repetitions of a positive experience create an identification with the object as a reliable source of pleasurable release, and the expectation that future experiences will be equally satisfactory. Likewise an unpleasant experience will encourage the child to avoid similar situations, resolving after sufficient repetitions in an inhibition and the deferral of the energy to another locus of the body where the force of the inhibited desire will either seek expression through an established object of desire or expend itself within the body—often as tension. Not all experiences with an object of desire will meet with the expected response. Instead of a smile and a hug, the child may be told not to interrupt. The inconsistency, initially confusing, requires that the child learn to differentiate contexts as well as objects. Within certain environments a cathexis will be reinforced, while not in others—the father is there; the father leaves. This ambivalence need not negate the object as a source of release but will necessitate the deferral of expenditure and the search for an alternative mode of expression and/or a substitute for the preferred object of desire—*fort/da*. Through the definition of objects, adaptations to shifting environments, and the modes of expression chosen in relation to the object and the context, the outlines of subjectivity are drawn. But it is not this simple.

The experiences with objects, the evaluations of returns, and the frequency of repetitions create hierarchies within the subject. Primary

objects are differentiated from secondary substitutes; objects of desire
are further categorized in relation to the types of release and expected
returns; and certain environments are perceived as being conducive to
certain types of behavior. The cathexis with a primary object is recognized through systems of representations, but more importantly the
significance of the attachment is understood by the satisfactory expenditure of energy along facilitated pathways—paths that define the contours of subjectivity. The intensities crossing the body without organs
will use privileged modes of expenditure determined by the needs
seeking expression and received information defining the external
environment. These contingencies will lead to a prioritization of behaviors, including physical gesture. Moreover, the reinforcement of expectations that certain objects will be present combined with the repetition
of specific types of experience will condition the body to adopt certain
behaviors, giving rise to habits—the repeated expression of energy in
forms that do not require conscious thought.

The significance of habit in the definition of the subject requires
further explication, but it must be approached indirectly. In situations
that require a conscious choice, either the circumstances or the available objects for the expenditure of energy do not fit what have become
normative expectations. The unexpected requires a redirection of energies, a concentration on the situation that makes us aware of the need
to decide. The body is more attuned to expenditure of force and feels it
more intensely. The experience results in a heightened awareness of
external responses to the decision because the unknown circumstances
make us feel particularly vulnerable. Therefore, modes of expenditure
requiring conscious thought are privileged over those that are habitual
and that can be utilized without special attention. This does not mean
acts of consciousness are of greater value in maintaining the well-being
of the body. Although habitual breaches require less energy to *effect*
discharge, this does not mean that less energy is expressed. A frequently facilitated path, with its virtual guarantee of release and
promise of "easy" repetition, provides greater, though less noticeable,
releases of energy. Indeed, the body organizes itself in order to maintain such conduits, and when circumstances challenge the use of a
habitual path, anxiety is induced, bringing the situation to consciousness. A conflict between a habitual mode of behavior and external circumstances will constellate choices designed to reconfigure the environment and its objects so that traditional modes of behavior can be

maintained. This is particularly true if the existing conditions appear to demand behavioral relativity, to call into question preferred objects of desire or necessitate permanent shifts in accepted environments. Subjectivity depends primarily on habitual, ingrained forms of release. The preferred circumstances are those where the objects of desire are available for the expenditure of energy along facilitated neural pathways, and where the external environment supports the subject's preferred modes of expression.

As the need for objects and a supportive context indicate, subjectivity depends on reciprocity: subjects, in addition to expecting a pleasurable return from their own patterns of release, need to accept the role of object and support the patterns of expression demanded by others. Social systems arise because of the failure to establish reciprocal relations, and because of the inequities inherent in this failure and the assumed right of one group to privilege their needs over those of others. For "she" of Not I there is a failure in reciprocity; she exists but is consistently unable to define a system of expenditures that will allow for an affirmation of her subjectivity. "So no love . . . spared that . . . no love such as normally vented on the . . . speechless infant . . . in the home . . . no . . . nor indeed for that matter any of any kind . . . no love of any kind . . . at any subsequent stage" (Beckett 1984, 216). The repeated absence of an object of desire and any pleasurable return from expenditures of energy creates a negative expectation, and a displacement of need from loving modes of release onto other types of behavior. The absence of reciprocity limits how she can express her needs, and therefore her ability to function in society. Moreover, these limits define her position in the system of social hierarchies. Outcast at birth, she remains outcast, defining the conditions of her existential solitude. But her isolation is existential only for her; for the rest of the community she serves the purpose of marking the boundaries of acceptable social behavior.

Social systems require a periphery, margins of opposition that help reinforce an ideological hegemony, that provide a reason to conserve structures of power within the community. She is socially constructed, for the community, as a passive reminder of the threat posed by antisocial elements—her humiliation becoming a definition of the limits on acceptable behavior. It falls to her (though it seems to be her fate) to live on the margins of society; and there she must try, and largely fail, to construct her subjectivity, the means by which she succeeds (or fails) in satisfying her needs. However, it would be inaccurate to say that no reciprocity exists. Her modes of venting energy, inadequate as they may be, are encouraged by the *negative* responses she receives from the community. She has discovered that her patterns of behavior can produce experiences that satisfy needs. Unable to defend herself when accused of committing a crime, she fulfills society's need to reinforce moral behavior, "that time in court . . . what had she to say for herself . . . guilty or not guilty . . . stand up woman . . . speak up woman . . . stood there staring into space," and *her* need for human contact, "glad of the hand on her arm" (Beckett 1984, 221). Had she been able to speak, she might not have experienced even the minimal pleasure provided by the physical contact. Likewise, her inability or refusal to talk when purchasing items from the store describes an image antithetical to social propriety, while freeing her from experiencing the displeasure of being rejected.

> even shopping . . . out shopping . . . busy shopping centre . . . supermart . . . just hand in the list . . . with the bag . . . old black shopping bag . . . then stand there waiting . . . any length of time . . . middle of the throng . . . motionless . . . staring into space . . . mouth half open as usual . . . then pay and go . . . not as much as good-bye (219)

Inscribed as society's "other," she gives pleasure by embodying the inverse of the dominant ideology, which is the only source of "pleasure" she knows.

She does not exist completely outside the bounds of society, however. Margins define the interior limits of a structure; there must be a degree of inclusion, a sense of belonging, that keeps her from simply being elsewhere. To an extent she is there because of her apparent inability to imagine being anywhere else, but she is also there because the world in which she lives provides her pleasure—a hand on the arm. Her complicity with the society that marks her as a pariah is affirmed by the significant investment she has been taught to make in religion, "she fixing with her eye . . . a distant bell . . . as she hastened towards it . . . fixing it with her eye . . . lest it elude her" (Beckett 1984, 218). Her fixation on the bell, her fear of losing it, acknowledges its status as an object of desire that implicitly promises expenditure. The connection between faith in God and the return of love was learned at the same time, and in the same circumstances, that cathexes with other people as positive objects of desire were repressed, "brought up as she had been to believe . . . with the other waifs . . . in a merciful . . . God" (217). The displacement, encouraged in childhood, offers up the promise of nothing less than salvation—not as a metaphysical potential, but as a very real and physical liberation. "God is love . . . tender mercies . . . new every morning" (221–22). Implicit in the promise is renewal, a rebirth distanced from the frustration and suffering imposed upon her by a callous and indifferent society.

But the "tender mercies," the privileged release, come at a cost. To be saved she must willingly embrace a further system of resistances that places strict limitations on her behavior. "The individual *is interpellated as a (free) subject in order that [she] shall submit freely to the commandments of the Subject, i.e., in order that [she] shall (freely) accept [her] subjection. . . . There are no subjects except by and for their subjection*" (Althusser 1971, 182). Explicit within the ideology of salvation is the codification of the law that makes the satisfactory release of desire contingent upon the valuation of certain modes of behavior. Acquired resistance to the selection of certain objects of desire is a condition that must be met if she can hope to find ultimate release. Failure to make the correct choices threatens the loss of the Subject, forcing her to interpret negatively otherwise positive effractions, causing an inversion of what may be pleasurable into what *is* painful, "that notion of punishment . . . for some sin or other . . . or for the lot . . . or no particular reasons . . . for its own sake . . . thing she understood perfectly . . . that notion of punishment" (Beckett 1984, 217). Suffering as a way of life, as the appropriate definition of her "lot in life," perpetually postpones the expenditure, or allows its release only through the anticipation of a future satisfaction. The pathways effracted that lead her to move toward the bell—the fetishized substitute for the promised-but-never-present object of desire—activate an expression of energy of such magnitude that it is equaled only by the dread that an inhibition will be imposed, that the metonymic symbol will be spirited away, that punishment for some sin—real or imaginary—will be exacted.

However, as Joseph Smith points out, her faith is not simply the effects of politics, but bespeaks a nostalgia that "*can* be the mourning of everyday life, the ordinary, ongoing grief pertaining to the daily encounter with past, present and anticipated loss" (1991, xxiii). She remembers the pleasure encountered in the promise of faith, and in that remembering experiences a similar pleasure; and fearing its loss, "she hastened towards it . . . fixing it with her eye . . . lest it elude her" (Beckett 1984, 218). The release of tension arising from the deferral of need is so infrequent that she must savor the memory, sustain the moment, and pursue the image lest it escape her forever. Nevertheless, her desire, its inflections as grief, and the complex and contradictory "pleasures" experienced by the body help to secure the boundaries of her abjection.

The resistances that constrict her social behavior also limit her ability to experience herself. She is able neither to experience pleasure nor find release through tears.

> one evening on the way home . . . sitting staring at her hand . . . there in her lap . . . palm upward . . . suddenly saw it wet . . . the palm . . . tears presumably . . . hers presumably . . . no one else for miles . . . no sound . . . just the tears . . . sat and watched them dry . . . all over in a second. (Beckett 1984, 220–21)

The uncertainty she experiences when confronted with tears, her insensate body and the detachment with which she observes the event, serves Beckett's seeming desire to negate the body, but it also describes the effects of social practices that define marginality. Only excessive frustration resulting from her inability to express herself can create a force of sufficient magnitude to disrupt normal patterns of resistance, whether as tears or the sudden eruption of language. "sudden urge to . . . tell . . . then rush out stop the first she saw . . . nearest lavatory . . . start pouring it out . . . steady stream . . . mad stuff . . . half the vowels wrong . . . no one could follow" (222). The intensity of her frustration forces a breach—a defecation of desire—in a language known only to herself but understood by no one. The experience becomes excruciatingly painful after the release, with the return of the prohibition. "till she saw the stare she was getting . . . then die of shame . . . crawl back in" (222). The return of a resistance to speaking signifies a reduction in the energy that led to the disruption. She could not have stopped sooner; but the shame she experiences at being seen behaving in an antisocial manner strengthens the inhibition, reinforcing her marginality and the belief that life is suffering.

It would be possible to stop here and begin a summary of the theory of subjectivity outlined—the processes of expenditure, the effect of
external circumstances on the expression of desire. But to do so would
deny my complicity in her marginalization, because I echo the Mouth,
"what? . . . who? . . . no! . . . she!" (Beckett 1984, 217). She is not I. Despite
my empathy (pity?), I do not confuse myself with her. She remains
"other," as she does for the narrator, the disembodied mouth. There are
pleasures in these categorizations of the "other" that need to be
explored because they are the pleasures of subjectivity.

She is someone who picks flowers and goes shopping, who follows
the sound of a bell, who speaks uncontrollably, who is accused of committing crimes, who is unable to feel pleasure and who finds it difficult
to cry. She is a victim, deserted by her parents, unloved in the home,
imprisoned for a crime she may not have committed. She is irrational,
breaking into incomprehensible diatribes in front of strangers. She is
frigid, unable to feel pleasure or pain. She is passive, needing to be
aroused to experience pleasure, following the object of her desire rather
than seeking it out. She is the "other" who is acted upon but is not an
agent on her own behalf. She is what the Mouth needs her to be, an
object on which it can release the intensities of its desire.

A satisfactory conclusion to the Mouth's cathexis can be guaran-
teed because the "other" is not an object but an object in language. The
attributes selected, the signs activated to specify the "she," create a narrative that defines her. This context indicates patterns of facilitation
within the speaking subject that insure minimal resistance, habits of
consciousness that privilege particular scenarios. In fact, the actual,
material existence of the "she" is inconsequential because the image is
sufficiently vivid to satisfy the requirements for release. The privilege
granted her is, however, a ruse, because the Mouth does not need her
for herself. Rather she creates a context that vouchsafes the "I." She is
the landscape against which the analytic of sonorities is played out, in
which the struggle for subjectivity takes place. Like the body and material reality in Not I, she is negated, relegated to the peripheries of the
discourse, subjected but not subject.

She is a key to unraveling the mystery, to locating a missing person: those aspects of the self that I cannot know, but in my thirst for
self-understanding desire to know. To give way to this desire is to
reproduce the tendency in modern thought to feminize the unknowable in subjectivity.

> Right across the spectrum of contemporary Continental and espe-
> cially French philosophy the "feminine" functions as a powerful
> vehicle to convey the critical attempts to redefine human subjec-
> tivity. . . . the feminization of thought seems to be prescribed as a
> fundamental step in the general programme of anti-humanism
> which marks our era. (Braidotti 1987, 236)

The appropriation of the female to represent the other-that-is-I parallels
the use of "she" as a landscape against which the problem of the subject
is argued. She is an image that is defined only to be absorbed as the
background. The face, critiqued by Deleuze and Guattari as the
despotic construction of *signifiance* and subjectivity, is transcribed
within the landscape.

> All faces envelop an unknown, unexplored landscape; all land-
> scapes are populated by a loved or dreamed-of face, develop a face
> to come or already past. What face has not called upon the land-
> scapes it amalgamated, sea and hill; what landscape has not
> evoked the face that would have completed it, providing an unex-
> pected complement for its lines and traits? (Deleuze and Guattari
> 1987, 172–73)

As the "other," "she" does not define the limits of subjectivity but
inscribes the parameters, the closure of representation within which
the subject must be conceived. She is the mirror in which I seek my lost
self.

I am not the landscape "she" is; I do not lack a body. I can act
through my agency, or the illusion of it, which mitigates the impact of
the despair encountered in Beckett, though it also defines it. This position is not available to her, nor to the female reader. In the definition of
the subject, "she" is equated with both the "I" and the "not I," without
difference or distinction. She represents but is neither the mystery I
cannot unravel, nor the material body. There is no room for her within
this configuration to define a subject position, since she is merely a figure peripheral to the discourse of the self.

> The enigma that *is* woman will therefore constitute the *target*, the
> *object*, the *stake*, of a masculine discourse, of a debate among men,
> which would not consult her, would not concern her. Which, ulti-

mately, she is not supposed to know anything about. (Irigaray 1985, 13)

For me it is different because I am not "she," but "he," who, with the knowledge gained from her, can assess my own subjectivity in response to the existential dilemma posited by Beckett. I am the authorized reader, spectator, because, and only because, I am "he," "having vanished . . . thin air . . . no sooner buttoned up his breeches" (Beckett 1984, 216). She is not so fortunate; she is trapped within the text without the right of refusal.

A reserve supply of negativity sustaining the articulation of their moves, or refusals to move, in a partly fictional progress toward the mastery of power. Of knowledge. In which she will have no part. Off-stage, off-side, beyond representation, beyond selfhood. (Irigaray 1985, 22)

If the pain I feel in *Not I* is real, then so is the pleasure I receive, which arises, at least in part, from the images of an abused woman used to evoke my despair. However, my pleasure lies not in her violation but in her marginalization. Locating her in the peripheries of society is acceptable to me because it defines her exclusion from a community of subjects in which I am included. Her abjection defines my privilege. It allows me to contemplate the existential distress experienced at the untransgressable limits of subjectivity within the comforts of a discourse that reinscribe my belief that I can exercise the power of agency within a dominant, if not hegemonic, male structure.

Subjectivity is determined by the pathways developed within the body for the "safe" expression of energy. It is an ongoing system of shifting intensities that resists narrativization, or at least closure and evaluation. It is, in this sense, neutral; it is a process. What makes subjectivity problematic are the forces that encourage specific modes of expression, and the effects the canalization of energy has on other bodies.

Interventions into the world depend upon a movement of energy within the body, whose origins are unimportant but whose function is necessary to the health of the physical being. For Freud, this force arises from the instincts and defines the libido; while for Beckett, it is "the buzzing . . . so-called . . . in the ears . . . though not of course actually . . .

not in the ears at all . . . in the skull . . . dull roar in the skull" (Beckett 1984, 217–18). Deleuze and Guattari utilize Artaud's concept of "the body without organs."

> Nothing here is representative; rather, it is all life and lived experience: the actual, lived emotion . . . A harrowing, emotionally overwhelming experience, which brings the schizo as close as possible to matter, to a burning, living center of matter. (Deleuze and Guattari 1983, 19)

Each plays with the same paradox. They attempt to localize the force—in the instincts, the skull, the center of matter—through a trope that resists localization. Where do the instincts reside? From where in the skull does the "dull roar" emanate, or is it only *experienced* in the skull? We are brought as "close as possible" to a center, but always at a distance, perpetually *de*centered. The implication in each is that this force is in the body, throughout the body—in the passage of chemical impulses across synapses, relaying stimulations across perceptual surfaces and reflexive tissues—not in an undifferentiated flow, but according to "bands of intensity, potentials, thresholds, and gradients," respondent to the needs of the body at any particular moment. And its passing is not indiscriminate, but along semipermeable channels defined by the organization of the body and its functions.

The movement of energy is continuous but not uniform, occurring simultaneously in different localities and at varying intensities throughout the body. Quantitative differences will fluctuate depending upon immediate contingencies. The need for greater amounts of blood in a particular part of the body, for instance, will be communicated by an increase in the number of activations within and across particular networks. These effects are not autonomous but alter other environments in the body, necessitating adjustments in other intensities. This is not to imply that increases in quantities are matched by decreases elsewhere. There can be no assumption of a normative balance that must be maintained. There is no center, no central bank tracking debits and credits. Rather there are interconnecting flows that influence one another, but that have their own integrity as defined by the body *with* organs.

Movements of energy through the body are not identical but carry a valence, not in the sense of positive or negative charges, but rather whether an intensity signifies an attraction or repulsion.

Where do these pure intensities come from? They come from the
two preceding forces, repulsion and attraction, and from the opposition of these two forces. It must not be thought that the intensities
themselves are in opposition to one another, arriving at a state of
balance around a neutral state. On the contrary, they are all positive in relationship to the zero intensity that designates the full
body without organs. (Deleuze and Guattari 1983, 19)

This is what is significant in the configuration set forth by Deleuze and
Guattari: the fluctuating gradients of energy are not in opposition with
one another but are equally positive in the functioning of the body. The
question of negativity does not exist in the realm of the real but enters
into the lexicon of experience only with the introduction of representations and the possibility of interpretation. Were negativity to precede
consciousness, the body without organs would be an impossibility; as
would the libido of Freud and the buzzing of Beckett.

There is, however, a danger in this conceptualization. Derrida, in
"The Mystic Writing Pad," follows Freud in labeling this process
"breaching." The term carries with it implications of resistance and
transgression that imply not only a degree of violence but transform
the process into a power relationship. The movement of force through
the body cannot be seen as an act of violation, which carries with it an
inescapable negativity; but the aggregation of a charge sufficient to
allow for movement within the system. The utilization of neural pathways is a natural function and ought to be viewed in terms of compatibility rather than aggression.

This cooperative conceptualization of the dynamics of desire in the
body is most nearly figured by a newborn, whose existence can be
defined in terms of liquids; the streaming of milk, blood, tears, urine,
and feces. All move through the body, not in continuous flows, but
sequenced according to attained thresholds, degrees of expenditure,
divergences and confluences: "everywhere there are breaks-flows out
of which desire wells up" (Deleuze and Guattari 1983, 37). Desire wells
up because a break in the flow does not result in a reservoir of unex-
pended energy, unless it is a momentary delay until a sufficient charge
is obtained for another repetition, nor does it resolve itself in complete
expenditure: "everything functions at the same time, but amid hiatuses
and ruptures, breakdowns and failures, stalling and short circuits, distances and fragmentations, within a sum that never succeeds in bring-

ing its various parts together so as to form a whole" (Deleuze and Guattari 1983, 42). There is always an excess of force whose expression is deferred and alternative avenues of expression are optioned. This is all possible without an assumption of violence. Once a pathway has been utilized for the reduction of the omnipresent surplus of demand, be it only for the creation of body tensions, it will continue to be a cooperative and expressive alternative.

Were the body a closed system, a homeostasis might be possible; but the continual influx of perceptual data and the need to influence external environments result in continually shifting levels of intensity. Interactions with worlds outside of the body have a significance beyond the accumulation or depletion of energy, however. For Lacan, the process of subjectification is initiated in the mirror stage: the moment at which the body is recognized as distinct within the field of vision and a relationship between background and foreground is established. The ability to isolate an image of the self is a partial resolution of the body's attempts to reconcile the destabilizing effects of separation from the source of nurturing and the neural development that makes possible the beginnings of cognition. The feelings generated by consciousness of an "other" give rise to pleasurable sensations within disparate parts of the body. A connection is made between perception and physical responses that establishes an expectation that similar events will initiate equally enjoyable experiences. The *knowledge* that the perceptions of the body can be pleasurable encourages the continued interaction, now as a conscious act.[1] It is no longer part of a flow of intensities, but a canalization, a structuring of the body for the purpose of pleasurable expenditures.

The specification of a pathway as a means to pleasure makes it attractive to other energies seeking expenditure. Those which are activated and received with pleasurable responses become associated with the image of the self and, therefore, serve as nascent self-identifications.

> It is a strange subject, however, with no fixed identity, wandering about over the body without organs, but always remaining peripheral to the desiring-machines, being defined by the share of the product it takes for itself, garnering here, there, and everywhere a reward in the form of a becoming or an avatar, being born of the states that it consumes and being reborn with each new state. "It's me, and so it's mine." (Deleuze and Guattari 1983, 16)

Those excitations that receive painful responses or are located in the matrix of repulsion must seek expression elsewhere. This does not mean these energies are not integral in the formation of the subject, but that they will become implicated in other structures, such as a rigidification in those parts of the body where displeasure is experienced. Such constructions should not be perceived as negative, but as the ways in which the body responds to particular events.

Who I am, then, will depend on the intensity of the impulse, the channel selected, the action resulting from the movement of force through the body and perceptual responses to the stimulation. If the result is pleasurable, the pathway is utilized repeatedly until it becomes habitual; if painful, chemical resistances eventually develop within the neural cells that make using the route virtually impossible, and alternatives must be located. In the latter instance a repression is created, a blockage that prohibits repetitions of expenditure through a particular structure. This does not mean the charge is stopped; rather, it is deferred onto other avenues that offer opportunities for a successful expenditure. When the exterior world begins to resist these expressions by sending unpleasurable responses, and no suitable alternative is available, the movement of the force becomes internalized. It is in the interaction with environments outside the body that we are able to interpret our behaviors and that concepts of negativity enter into our interaction with the world.

Within this process the flows circulating within the body increasingly encounter obstacles to movement. Dams and gates, levies are constructed that restrict the options for expression. The fluidity of the body without organs becomes rigidified and channeled. Impulsive responses to stimulations are denied free access to the body's surface and must negotiate a labyrinth of behavioral options until a pathway or a combination of pathways are found that will allow for expenditure, for pleasure. The complexity of the neural narrative—the twists and turns involved in the movement from impulse to expression—is not the effect of the body's organization, but of the system of checks and balances that arises from the process of socialization, the interpretations of external responses to behaviors. This complex movement of force through the body allows for the expression of energy and is what Beckett, in *Not I*, refers to as the streaming, as desire. But these streams are constrained by the effects of experience that resist fluidity of motion and mold it into controlled responses. The systems of rigidification that develop will reflect interactions with the community in which the subject lives; and the degree to which these are habituated will determine the quantity of energy expended along these pathways and the pleasure experienced through these modes of expression.

This is both the pessimism and optimism of subjectivity. Subjectivity, in the last instance, is the manifestation of the flow of intensities, the ways in which they are channeled, and the resulting articulations of desire. This movement is irrepressible, and once a pathway has proven to offer a satisfactory means of expression, constructing a repression, a prohibition, is virtually impossible and cannot be done without damage to the body—*unless* alternative modes of pleasure are found to replace undesirable, culturally supported habits. Change is possible, but extremely difficult. It cannot be done through repression, which will only engender resistance and exacerbate relations of power, but through the rearticulation of pleasure.

Repressions and prohibitions, as Klaus Theweleit has shown in *Male Fantasies,* do not lead to more positive relations between people or within the body, but to fascism and an intensification of violence.

> The body was so kept in check with pain; the whip migrated into the hands of an "educator." When he approached a woman, this kind of man was already a hard, solid ship, incapable of experiencing mingling with another body as a pleasurable expansion and reordering of boundaries. (Theweleit 1987, 322)

If relations between genders, or for that matter with people of color and different ethnic groups, are to be freed from the bonds of oppression that now define them; the question of desire must be seen in terms of maintaining a fluidity within the subject, not rigidification and resistance to the flows of intensity. Repression does not stop the movement of energy but diverts it into other forms of expression.

> Yet what the masses (all of us, that is) suffer most from are "false" *feelings*, feelings that are perverted, alienated from their goals, and turned into their opposites. . . . The real problem is that our bodies cramp up when they try to feel pleasure; sweat breaks out where love should; our soft, erect members become unsatisfied bones; our desire to penetrate another person's body becomes a lethal act; and contact between two sets of skin, two bodies, produces ten-

sion, dirt, and death, instead of release, purification, and rebirth. (Theweleit 1987, 416–17)

This is not a call for the untrammeled release of desire. Such a dream is impossible. Freeing of demand would merely mean the use of already existing networks of expression that would resolve themselves, as they do currently, in forms of oppression. What is needed is the means to be fluid, to express desire in ways that are constructive, that open channels rather than constructing dams or releasing floods.

I have outlined this model of energy flows within the body in part to insist upon the complexity of the system and to resist perceiving subjectivity as merely an effect of cognitive functions that inevitably places emphasis on the products of consciousness rather than physical processes. I do not wish to claim that this model adequately describes the experience of subjectivity or the limits of a utopic vision of what it means to be a subject, quite the contrary. The subject is defined by a configuring of the body, a rigidification of the boundaries within which energy flows, in response to interactions within socially constructed environments.

The question is how to locate new modes of expression in bodies that are constructed *to maintain* forms that are oppressive, how to develop new habits for the pleasurable release of energy that will not objectify the "other" but allow her to experience the same pleasurable release of energy in terms of the demands of her body rather than ours.

Jürgen Habermas, in his reading of George Herbert Mead's theory of subjectivity, offers a third term to offset the tendency to perceive subjectivity as an oscillation between negativities of existentialism and postmodernism and the cultural inscriptions of ideology. The term he locates in the pragmatics of his postmetaphysics is *intersubjectivity*.

> The turn to an intersubjectivistic way of looking at things leads in the matter of "subjectivity" to a surprising result: the consciousness that is centered, as it seems, in the ego is not something immediate or purely inward. Rather, self-consciousness forms itself on the path from without to within, through the symbolically mediated relationship to a partner in interaction. (Habermas 1992, 177)

The necessity of others in the definition of the self and the determination of action—its possibilities and potential efficacy—is not perceived by Habermas as a resolution to the binary of individual and society; rather, it describes the occluded ground on which the binary is constructed. The "symbolically mediated relationship to a partner in interaction" of intersubjectivity is the ground to be regained, because it is across this terrain that we negotiate differences, that we construct obstacles to communication and therefore understanding. By "regaining" I do not mean an act of reterritorialization; that would be unnecessary—it is already territorialized. Instead I mean an opening of spaces, an ecology of reclamation that allows for a valuing of differences within intersubjective relations.

NOTES

This chapter is a revised version of an essay that first appeared in Joseph H. Smith, ed., *The World of Samuel Beckett* (Baltimore: Johns Hopkins University Press, 1991).
1. Infants do recognize shifts in the field of perception and experience pleasure when a parent's face enters the live of vision, or displeasure when the image disappears. Nor am I firmly wedded to Lacan's moment of the mirror stage as the first moment of consciousness. I use it merely as a metaphor for the inciting incident which makes conscious differentiation within the field possible.

Chapter 6

Hearing Voices

What I want to ask is, Are we able to have an ethics of acts and their pleasures which would be able to take into account the pleasure of the other.

(Foucault 1983, 233)

The movement toward abjection implies a careful and incremental deconstruction of all structures of privilege and value. It is a rending of the fabric of subjectivity, a tearing of the weave that provides us pleasure in ourselves, and an immanent loss of self-worth in the absence of meaning. Such an act can resolve itself into immobility and despair; or a reconsideration of our privileges can, with no less despair, initiate a movement toward re-evaluating the ways in which we interact with others that permits the formation of new habits or a re-privileging of the existing repertoire. Patterns of behavior can be constructed differently to allow for a different understanding of the choices we make and the effects of those decisions. Such changes do not imply a new subjectivity, but an alteration of existing behaviors that can redefine the ways in which we approach each other—what Foucault calls an ethics "able to take into account the pleasure of the other."

Heiner Müller and Hamletmachine

No one has questioned his privilege and its costs with more excruciating vigilance than Heiner Müller. Rejecting the capitalism of the West after the Second World War, Müller chose to live in East Germany despite repeated opportunities to defect. A dedicated communist, he nevertheless recognized the repressive nature of Stalinism during the suppression of the Hungarian revolution in 1956. The effects of this contradiction—his devotion to communism and his hatred of the fascist state—figure in his 1977 play, *Hamletmachine.* In this work a parallel is developed between the influence Shakespeare's *Hamlet* has exerted on Müller's development as a writer and the effect of Stalin on his political relationship to the East German government. Both are perceived as formative in determining who he has become and as tyrannical forces from which he would like to escape. Between the poles of this binary, Müller envisions himself as Hamlet ("Hamlet-machine = H. M. = Heiner Müller. I carefully disseminated this interpretation" [Müller 1984, 51]) and Ophelia as a representative of the radical Left and feminism trying to escape from under the yoke of repressive patriarchal systems, whether Shakespeare, Stalin, or Hamlet. It is in exploring the relationship between Hamlet and Ophelia, between Heiner Müller and the communities she represents, that the playwright undertakes "a self-critique of the intellectual . . . the description of a petrified hope, an effort to articulate a despair so it can be left behind" (Müller 1984, 50).

For Heiner Müller, as for Hamlet, this means the despair of inaction in the face of tyranny, but for Shakespeare's character this questioning is an exploration of the possibility of self-deception and the doubt that rational thought can deal with the impossible. Müller confronts a postmodern subjectivity, one defined by self-deception and the failure of reason, one where the issue is not choosing between action and inaction, but determining whether action is possible in a world where subjectivity is fragmented and multiple. It is not simply "to be or not to be" but "to be or to be or to be . . ." In the act of deconstructing *Hamlet,* in releasing the play resisted by the metaphors, Müller seeks the constructions of pleasure and memory in his own history so that he can define tropes that will adequately communicate his own despair. He wishes to account for his own complicity with atrocity—both as a German and a communist—and to understand how he finds himself occupying positions he abhors, seemingly against his will.

In this approach to *Hamletmachine* (there are many others), I will focus on two central images. One is the final image of the play: Ophelia, from a wheelchair, promises acts of terror while "two men in white smocks wrap gauze around her and the wheelchair, from bottom to top" (Müller 1984, 58). The second is Hamlet/Müller's description of a revolutionary uprising:

> My place, if my drama would still happen, would be on both sides
> of the front, between the frontlines, over and above them. I stand

in the stench of the crowd and hurl stones at policemen soldiers tanks bullet-proof glass. I look through the double doors of bullet-proof glass at the crowd pressing forward and smell the sweat of my fear. Choking with nausea, I shake my fist at myself who stands behind the bullet-proof glass. Shaking with fear and contempt, I see myself in the crowd pressing forward, foaming at the mouth, shaking my fist at myself. (56)

Through a reading of the silencing of Ophelia and Hamlet's schizophrenic experience we come to understand Müller's critique of the intellectual and his despair; and yet we can also perceive the outlines of a necessity that may allow us to avoid the petrifying inertia of pessimism.

Müller's Ophelia is not crippled by madness, nor does she commit suicide. This is the Ophelia "the river didn't keep" (54); this is the woman whose despair at the loss of a lover and the death of her father does not lead to insanity and the end of her life.

Yesterday I stopped killing myself. I'm alone with my breasts my thighs my womb. I smash the tools of my captivity, the chair the table the bed. I destroy the battlefield that was my home. I fling open the doors so the wind gets in and the scream of the world. I smash the window. With my bleeding hands I tear the photos of the men I loved and who used me on the bed on the table on the ground. I set fire to my prison. I throw my clothes into the fire. I wrench the clock that was my heart out of my breast. I walk into the street clothed in my blood. (54–55)

Clothed in her blood, Ophelia, in Müller's drama, refuses to be the landscape upon which the battle for the rights of the father takes place; refuses to be merely a victim of Hamlet's madness, of Claudius's need to know the cause of Hamlet's affliction. Instead, Ophelia rises up against the oppression of her sex.

I take back the world I gave birth to. I choke between my thighs the world I gave birth to. I bury it in my womb. Down with the happiness of submission. Long live hate and contempt, rebellion and death. When she walks through your bedrooms carrying butcher knives you'll know the truth. (58)

Ophelia takes on the role of the avenging Electra. No longer willing to accept the river as her end, she becomes a terrorist—Ulriche Meinhoff and Squeaky Fromme, whose words she speaks. She is the revolutionary who, because of her abjection, has nothing to lose—not even her life, since it has been taken from her and constructed by men, by Müller/Shakespeare.

Shakespeare, in writing the Ophelia-the-river-takes, confined her to the margins of theater history; but given agency and consciousness, her story is very different. It tells of the violent necessity of change. In *Hamletmachine*, Müller displaces the dialectic of historical materialism from the axis of class conflict to the repression of sexual difference; and locates the potential for radical action in the lives of those most persistently oppressed and ideologically dispossessed. In *Hamlet*, this person is Ophelia. But Müller is not optimistic: at the end of the play there are two men in white smocks with gauze.

The enshrouding of Ophelia, the binding of the voice of the other, is an extremely powerful image, and a metaphor for the predominant response of those in power to the threat of radical change. Müller, however, does not displace this response onto others, but recognizes it as a central contradiction in his own life. It is this point of resistance that Müller critiques so rigorously in *Hamletmachine*: recognition of the need for change does not necessarily mean a willingness to change.

Clothed in blood, Ophelia walks out into the street. Müller/Hamlet's uprising, "if it still would happen," "starts with a stroll" (Müller 1984, 56). "The street belongs to the pedestrians" (56). A fellow traveler, Müller/Hamlet joins Ophelia: overturning cars, sweeping armed police out of the way, crying for the overthrow of the government, storming the government building with stones. But there is a limit to how far he can go, because he recognizes himself on the other side of the bulletproof glass door; he perceives his complicity with the state. To topple the system would be to destroy himself. "To be or not to be" is once again the question. Indeed it is his awareness of this contradiction that defines the self-criticism of *Hamletmachine*.

One explanation for Müller's complicity with the repressiveness of the German Democratic Republic, one that Müller does not shy from confronting, is the question of privilege. Despite official reluctance to allow productions of his works in the East, Müller was granted access to the West and traveled with relative freedom to work in the United States and Europe; the taxes on this income were considerably reduced;

and he lived among the cultural elite with access to Western goods. But Müller was acutely aware of the cost of these liberties: "In the solitude of airports / I breathe again I am / A privileged person My nausea / Is a privilege / Protected by torture / Barbed wire Prisons" (Müller 1984, 57). While it would be naive to deny the compensatory value of these freedoms, to say that the pleasures derived from "selling out" explain his complicity with the suffering of others would be extremely cynical and self-serving. We need to look further.

The metaphor of the bulletproof glass door that separates Müller from himself during the imagined uprising resonates with other auto-biographical images of separation. The first is through an open door-way:

> Through the crack I saw how a man was hitting my father in the face. . . . I lay in bed when the door to my room opened. My father stood in the door, behind him the strangers, big, in brown uniforms. . . . I hear him softly call my name. I didn't answer and lay very still. (Müller 1989, 27)

Separated from his father, who was arrested by the Nazis for involvement with the Social-Democratic Party of Germany (a communist organization), Müller was aware of his implicit betrayal and the cost of silence. This moment was repeated soon after when he and his mother visited the prison, where his father "couldn't touch our hands through the narrow wire mesh. I had to step very close to the gate to see his thin face completely" (Müller 1989, 28). The image of his father was complicated when, released from prison and unemployed, he asked his son to write an essay praising Hitler so that he might find work (30); and again when his father emigrated to the West in 1951 "to disengage himself from the war of the classes," where he "found his peace years later . . . [paying] out pensions to murderers of workers and to widows of murderers of workers" (31). Heiner Müller refused to take part in this betrayal and remained in East Berlin. His last visit with his father replicates more precisely the image of a glass partition. Müller

> was led . . . through a long bright hallway to the glass door of the isolation ward. . . . We stood there, the glass between us, and looked at each other. His thin face was pale. We had to raise our voices when we talked. He rattled at the locked door. . . . He let his

arm drop, looked at me through the glass, and was silent. . . . When
I left, I saw him standing behind the glass door and waving. (32)

Each image deconstructs the others, making a concise formulation of
meaning impossible; but in the resonating associations, the concepts of
love and separation, commitment and betrayal, and speech and silence
reverberate.

On the streets is the son who recognizes the father's acts of
betrayal; behind the bulletproof glass is the son who embraces the
father with love. On one side is the communist who rejects the fascist
apparatus of the state; on the other is the communist who embraces the
state as the only possibility for creating a new order. The force of will is
clearly aligned with the desire for change, or Hamlet/Müller would
not be in the streets; but there is outside the force of will, another less
vocal but stronger construction of desire—the promised pleasure of
loving the father, of being true to the state.

Hamlet/Müller's position within *Hamletmachine* can be understood as a conflict between ingrained patterns of subjective response
(habits of consciousness) and the recognition of the need for change
(the promise of alternative pleasures). The desire to overthrow the state
(Claudius) for its betrayal of communism (the poisoning of King Hamlet) is placed in conflict with devotion to the state (defined by the rule
of the Father). The resolution of the conflict is not a rebellion, the
romantic dream of overthrowing the father/state, but the appearance
of two men in white smocks binding the voice of Ophelia. The unavoidable implication is that, when push comes to shove, the perpetuation of
habitual modes of expression, of expenditures that guarantee a pleasurable interpretation and the continuity of identity, will prevail over
an unwavering recognition of the necessity of change. The irreversibil-
ity of the contradiction locates the despair Müller wishes to articulate
and leave behind—the pain of recognition that in giving agency to
Ophelia, he continues to use her body as a landscape against which he
enacts his struggle, that it is not Hamlet who binds the voice of Ophelia, but Heiner Müller.

When Müller's Hamlet says, "I want to be a woman" (Müller 1984,
55) and is dressed as a prostitute, Müller acknowledges the degree to
which he has prostituted himself to the state, while he desires, like
Ophelia, to "wrench the clock that was my heart out of my breast"
(54–55). The clock, through the image of a Madonna on a swing, is

replaced by a cancerous breast. To rid himself of the cancer, Müller/Hamlet walks, in women's clothing, with Ophelia, but for him to dress as a woman is merely to parody her, to mimic the abject revolutionary the stream has tempted to suicide, a fact he confronts when he sees himself on the other side of the door. This is Müller's pessimism. In attempting to speak as Ophelia, he is mocking her suffering, reinforcing the structures of power that define her marginality. He is binding her voice.

Similarly, Stephen Heath, a member of the MLA panel "Men in Feminism," understands that the problem is not simply one of letting "Ophelia" speak, but of the need to incorporate his understanding of what she says. By *incorporating* I mean literally making it part of his body, because only if it works to modify behavior will it alter the contours of subjectivity. The first problem, however, is understanding what is being said. Heath recognizes a slippage in his own work, the tendency to ask, "What does feminism mean for men?" rather than "What is feminism?" (Heath 1987a, 27). The reflex to an economics of costs and returns inevitably distorts our understanding and allows us to deflect rather than embrace what is being said. Heath critiques his own essay, "Male Feminism," saying:

> The insistence in the piece on the political-ethical reality of feminism for men, for me-as-a-man (an insistence which I beli[e]ve to be important and needed, against the appropriative displacement of feminism into a set of ideas for a theoretical argument or a known politics, against men just assuming it is there for them to "go into," to have "positions" in, all the ways in which we avoid bringing it back questioningly onto ourselves) runs the risk of turning into a personal essentialism, outside any object, ethics separating from politics as *I* stop in silence. (Heath 1987a, 32)

The wrapping of Ophelia does more than silence her voice, it insists upon her absolute otherness; it defines the boundaries of her subjectivity. It permits Hamlet/Müller to perceive of himself as an existential subject, to slip into a solipsistic loop that allows him to indulge in the ethical implications of his position outside of her oppression while ignoring the politics of the gauze. He stops in silence.

What Heath and Müller ask, a question that reveals their pain, is how change can be effected when we continually fall prey to the traps of privilege. How do we, who are already on both sides of a bulletproof glass door, make possible a revolution that is against ourselves? It cannot be done in silence. But on what political-ethical ground do we act so that we do not merely reproduce the same?

The Space of Intersubjectivity

The metaphors are all spatial, having to do with positions that define difference and that are ultimately binary: here/there, subject/object, self/other, men/women, inside/outside. It would be simple to create with these binaries a model in which two circles, one labeled "self" and the second "other," are placed at a distance on a surface. This representation would denote the distinct individualism of each and the distance that must be bridged for communication to occur. Such an imaging would be disingenuous, however, not only because of its excessive simplicity, but because of its insistence on absolute difference between subjects. It disavows what I call the plane of similitude.

Similitude does not imply identity; it does not assume or expect that two subjects will be the "same." This plane is neither the uroboric state of undifferentiation, which Jung thought was the desired end of conscious beings, nor is it the body without organs described by Deleuze and Guattari, though it has more in common with the latter. Rather, it is a field that acknowledges difference. In fact, it is at its limits that we are able to begin to measure differences; or would be if its borders did not disintegrate in the liminal reaches of the unknowable, those aspects of the other we cannot experience. If the spatial metaphor with which I started were to be revised, the plane of similitude would be the crosshatched area of two overlapping circles, but circles lacking distinct edges, definitive boundaries.

This concept has antecedents in Foucault, Derrida, and Irigaray. For Foucault, the existence of similarity, if not identity, is necessary for the determination of difference; indeed, the knowledge of distinctions is based in "the empirical and murmuring resemblance of things, that unreacting similitude that lies beneath thought and furnishes the infinite raw material for divisions and distributions" (Foucault 1973, 58). In Derrida the transference of the gift, a noncognitive exchange of intensities, presupposes a field of interconnectedness that precedes differentiated interaction: "if there is a possible determination of subject—at that moment, there is no longer a gift. . . . there is no gift except in that all determinations . . . are absolutely unconscious and random" (Derrida 1987, 198). Irigaray also acknowledges a communication other than that made manifest in the processes of differentiation when she writes about the "dramatic relationships" to be discovered

> From the spaces between the figures, or stand-in figures. Spaces that organize the scene, blanks that sub-tend the scene's structuration and that will not yet be read as such. Or read at all? Not seen at all? Never in truth represented or representable, though this is not to say that they have no effect upon the present scenography. (1985, 137–38)

This field—which lies beneath thought, which passes intensities from one subject to another in a way that is absolutely unconscious and random, but which nevertheless effects the scenography—is that which allows us to experience each other, to mark and acknowledge differences between subjectivities.

It is this territory, this no man's land, that we so assiduously attempt to disavow or to deface beyond recognition when insisting upon the imprint of otherness, or failing that, to appropriate in a totalizing gesture the "right" to speak for all. The reasons for this intractable opposition to similarity have been extensively analyzed by those who are the victims of this persistent discrimination. What they seem to be saying is that there is a tendency to equate the experience of pleasure with the exercise of power, and that there is a prevalent belief that this is a prerogative of authority. There is a reluctance to acknowledging similarity because that would give others access to subjectivity and to power; and if they become the procreators of their own being, they may resist satisfying our needs when they are chosen to be the object of desire. Instead, we limit their mobility, maintain barriers against the force of change, in order to preserve habitual modes of self-satisfaction in the pursuit of what we have come to call pleasure. It is, as Foucault states, "a political ordering of life, not through an enslavement of others, but through an affirmation of self" (1980, 123). But enslavement is an unavoidable by-product of this affirmation, of this conception of the self.

The primary means for disavowing similitude are the use of direct violence and coercive ideologies; but the tools used are to be found, paradigmatically, in the avenues of perception and expression that define the body's externality. I will speak of four: touch, sight, speech, and hearing. In most instances these implements serve a double function. They permit the experience of pleasure and self-affirmation; and are a form of aggression that actively limits the mobility of the other. The relationship of touch to pleasure on the one hand, and to physical repression and objectification on the other, is sufficiently obvious that it need not detain us, except to acknowledge that this form of interpersonal contact is all too often extremely violent. Seeing, the fetishization of the other and the operations of the scopic drive as a means of denying subjectivity, has received intense scrutiny in the work of De Lauretis, Kaplan, and others; while Irigaray has located the solipsistic aspects of vision in the transposition of images: I take pleasure not in seeing the other but myself through the power and images "man has reflected there" (Irigaray 1985, 134). Sight operates to disenfranchise the other through the affirmation of self-reflection and the fragmentation of the other's body into consumable surfaces. The mouth offers a more overt form of subjugation because it keeps the other from speaking—or at least us from having to hear. At the same time, through the rhetoric of the voice, we appropriate the right to speak for the other. Marguerite Duras foregrounds this phenomenon in her description of the events of May 1968.

> They are the ones who started to speak, to speak alone and for everyone else, on behalf of everyone else, as they put it. They immediately forced women and extremists to keep silent. They activated the old language, enlisted the aid of the old way of theorizing, in order to relate, to recount, to explain this new situation. (1981, 111)

Through touch, sight, and voice, the other is excluded from the exercise of power, from expressing herself, because through each those in authority have found the means to affirm themselves as subjects and, by relegating others to the peripheries of discourse, limited the space in which "others" can seek their own affirmation.

The ear, however, has received somewhat less consideration; perhaps because the critique of the eye and the mouth, to say nothing of touch, leaves so little room for optimism. The ear *has* been subjected to critique. Luce Irigaray, in her deconstruction of the psychoanalytic process, writes:

> While all the while permissive, listening with benevolent neutrality, collecting, on a carefully circumscribed little stage, the interdict. The lines between the lines of discourse. But he restricts himself to reframing, re-marking, or "analyzing" its contours, re-stratifying its stages, so that order, good "conscious" order, may prevail. Elsewhere. (1985, 138)

Any attempt to understand what another is saying involves translation—the displacement and deferral of meaning resulting from disparities in subjectivity and experience. Irigaray's critique of Freud does not center on this inevitability, but on his failure to recognize the oppressive effect of his interpretation on the subjectivity of the other. In other words, Freud fails, as Benjamin states, "to admit that all translation is only a somewhat provisional way of coming to terms with the foreignness of languages" (1969, 75). To speak of the language of the other as being foreign is to recognize the difference between the intensities that gave rise to the expression and the dynamics of reception that are resolved in understanding. As Derrida points out, the attribution of meaning lies with the receiver. "It is the receiver who is the determining factor of the gift. . . . It is only the other, at the moment when it receives it, who decides the destination, and who says 'it is me who answers' or, 'it is mine'" (1987, 200). But in that moment of determination, in the listening to the intensities, meaning is supplied to the communication that defines the subjectivity of the sender. The order Freud seeks through the other is the order he wishes to find. The you I listen to is the you I want you to be.

This is not, however, the "truth" of communication, at least not the whole truth. In the process of listening, I have not understood all that you had to say, only that which I translated into my language. Within the communication I received there are other sounds, Barthes's grain of the voice, to which I chose not to listen. The act of selection leaves other intensities reverberating across the plane of similitude, which "is not to say that they have no effect upon the present scenography" (Irigaray 1985, 137–38). It is in these other sounds that I hear the ring of hope. But for the hope to be realized, I must relax my insistence on understanding you. Instead I must suspend the desire to know—a critical operation based on the definition of difference, the precision of meaning—and allow you to become *in*commensurate with my use of language, my system of differentiations. I must allow for the interplay of intensity without deciding whether it is a gift, whether I am the recipient. The *a*ffect, for there will be no certifiable effect, will not be knowledge of you or of myself, but of the plane of similitude and the unknowable fact of its existence. And in the pleasure of that moment I may recognize the value (to me) of your experience of subjectivity.

Underlying this theory is the assumption that the definition of, and avenues for, obtaining pleasure are determined by material practices. In brief, the field and technologies of desire are inscribed within the individual while socially prescribed modes of intercourse are becoming habitual. The effect of this social patterning is the construction of images of difference that raise barriers to the recognition of similarity, resulting in the marginalization of the other. To reverse this process, therefore, requires the acquisition of alternative practices, the first step of which is recognizing my own patterns of oppression.

To begin I must learn to hear rather than listen. When I listen to what another says I seek the "truth" of their statement, and in the evaluation of meaning place the speaker under scrutiny—I replicate through the ear the operations of the eye. And in the moment of reflection between reception and meaning, I define my relationship to others by defining my response to what they say. But if instead of *listening*, of positioning myself in judgment over what another has said, I defer the moment of decision, I can, perhaps, begin to experience the intensities of what is being said, to *hear*. To effect that moment of forbearance I must delay the attribution of meaning and focus instead on the parameters of differentiation I employ in making that attribution. By becoming self-conscious of my prejudices I can use them as a mirror in which to reflect not what another is saying, but the practices of objectification and marginalization I use in determining what they mean. If I can establish a resonance between what I hear and how I conceive of others, perhaps I will begin to hear the echoes of similitude that define our differences, and to attenuate the barriers I have constructed across the distance that separates us.

The cost of this self-reflection is a very real crisis of subjectivity, because it requires a willingness to endure the destabilized sense of self that arises from an interrogation of practices and a self-abjection that brings into question what it means to be. It means surrendering power to another; becoming, in the terms of Deleuze and Guattari, a minority, but one that does not assume the allegiance of another—hearing does not put an end to difference. But from this loss may arise a redefinition of pleasure—a pleasure located not in overcoming the resistance, but in experiencing the subjectivity of others, in witnessing their becoming.

Foucault and Ethics

Through this process may emerge the ethics Foucault was seeking at the end of his life: an aesthetics of subjectivity. In his last books, Foucault changes the subject of inquiry in *The History of Sexuality* from a genealogy of the mechanisms that produce systems of restraint and liberation to issues of sexual ethics. The locus of these historical explorations is the Hellenistic world prior to the ascendancy of Christianity as the predominant ethical system. The problematic he identifies in this period bears a striking resemblance to the difficulties faced today.

> Whereas formerly ethics implied a close connection between power over oneself and power over others, and therefore had to refer to an aesthetics of life that accorded with one's status, the new rules of the political game made it more difficult to define the relations between what one was, what one could do, and what one was expected to accomplish. (Foucault 1986, 84)

Far from constructing an argument for history repeating itself, I believe Foucault was seeking in the past a way of being that was both ethical and commensurate with the instabilities of a postmodern world—an ethics based not on a universal system of moral imperatives, but "an effort to affirm one's liberty and to give one's own life a certain form in which one could recognize oneself, be recognized by others, and in which even posterity could find an example" (Foucault 1989a, 311). The difficulty with the Graeco-Roman model and the Christian that succeeded it, and a trap for any ethics in a world dominated by issues of relativity, is the danger of solipsism.

> Whatever the new economy of bodies and pleasures, which Foucault seems to be hinting is about to appear, its ethical substance

may well be acts and pleasure/desire, and its telos may be an aesthetics of existence. But its content, its practices, cannot be the nonreciprocal practices of the Greeks, let alone the self-decipherment
and concern with purity essential to the Christian understanding
of human reality. (Dreyfus and Rabinow 1983, 263)

A theory concerned with ways of being must address the issue of reciprocity in relationships: care of the self is inextricably connected to care
for the other.

Conceptualizing a reciprocal relationship is not simply imagining
a balance between subjects who give and take, if for no other reason
than the difficulty in determining what to give and what is available to
be taken. Problems between men and women revolve around precisely
this issue. Assumptions of privilege and relations of power exacerbate
feelings of distrust rather than create an environment conducive to reciprocity. In a world without moral imperatives the question of locating
a basis on which to make ethical decisions is difficult but, nevertheless,
necessary. Foucault believes the self is the only possible ground for an
ethics; but he also understands that it is an extremely unstable
ground—which is both its virtue and its liability. The danger, of course,
lies in the ability of the subject to rationalize choices according to a
rhetoric of desire; that is, the promise of solipsistic pleasures can justify
nonreciprocal behaviors. The positive value of the subject as a site for
an ethics is that any subjectivity is "only one of the given possibilities of
organizing a consciousness of self" (Foucault 1989e, 330). Furthermore,
the organization of the subject as a conscious being "is constituted
through practices of subjection, or, in a more anonymous way, through
practices of liberation, of freedom . . . starting of course from a certain
number of rules, styles and conventions that are found in culture"
(Foucault 1989a, 313). The existence of alternative ways of organizing
consciousness and the potential for altering subjective practices and
resisting cultural administrations of behavior indicate the possibility of
transforming subjectivity, of redefining who we are as ethical beings.

It is in the interstices of ideology and at the intersections of experience that the possibility of choice exists. One of the decisions that can be
made, that was made in Antiquity, is to cultivate the self. "It [is] a question of making one's life into an object for a sort of knowledge, for a
techne—for an art" (Foucault 1983, 245). Articulating an aesthetics of
existence, defining oneself as an ethical being, becomes necessary when

society is in a state of flux and cannot offer, let alone maintain, a viable system of values. The absence of a morality by consensus requires "practices of the self" that "take the form of an art of the self, relatively independent of any moral legislation" (Foucault 1989b, 299). Self-mastery replaces obedience to an institutionally promulgated code of ethics. While the concept resonates harmonically with certain images of individualism, such a conclusion also gives us reason to pause because it reverberates equally well with solipsistic desires for the same.

The difficulty lies in determining a basis for deciding whether or not a particular choice is appropriate to the circumstances. This indeterminacy defines a pessimism because the lack of an external system of rules locates the ethical moment firmly within the subjective experience:

> it is the experience of a pleasure that one takes in oneself. The individual who has finally succeeded in gaining access to himself is, for himself, an object of pleasure. Not only is one satisfied with what one is and accepting of one's limits, but one "pleases oneself." (Foucault 1986, 66)

We are poised on the threshold of solipsism. It would be easy to succumb to the pleasures of the self, to enter the studios of *The Balcony* where it is possible to see the self "reflected a thousand times" (Genet 1966, 84). Such indulgence, while clearly pleasurable, is qualitatively different from the pleasure Foucault seeks in an aesthetics of existence. Caring for the self is not an immersion into endless repetitions of the same, but an art, *"techne,* that is to say, a practical rationality governed by a conscious goal" (Foucault 1989d, 276). The goal, as in all ethics, needs to be located in relations with others.

The decision-making process cannot be determined simply by self-reflection but through seeing the self *with* the other. Foucault develops this concept through a reading of Plato's *Alcibiades* and the metaphor of the eye.

> For Plato, one cannot simply look at oneself in a mirror. One has to look into another eye, that is, one *in* oneself, however in oneself in the shape of the eye of the other. And there, in the other's pupil, one will see oneself: the pupil serves as a mirror. (Foucault 1983, 249)

To see the self as seen by another is not as easy as it sounds. The eye of the other *"in* oneself" is a representation that will inevitably be distorted to configure more closely to the existing image of the self. Neither looking in nor using the eyes of the other as a mirror will give us access to ourselves, because ultimately we will be looking for the wrong things. The representation of the other must serve another purpose.

> To keep constant watch over one's representations . . . is not to inquire . . . concerning the deep origin of the idea that presents itself; it is not to try and decipher a meaning hidden beneath the visible representation; it is to assess the relationship between oneself and that which is represented. (Foucault 1986, 64)

To seek the deep structures of the self is to surrender to existential solipsism, to the inevitable vertigo experienced in the abyss of falling dreams. What needs to be sought in the eyes of the other is the relationship that exists between you and me.

In the exploration of intersubjectivity, the contours of the self will be placed in sharp relief; but to stop with the affirmation of identity is to fall prey to the traps of specularity, to miss the ethical moment. To look at the landscape against which the subject is foreground is to see a face. "For where he projects a . . . mirror to catch his reflection, he is already faced by another specularization. Whose twisted character is her inability to say what she represents" (Irigaray 1985, 134). As I look across the space of difference and attempt to define the limits, the details of *her* face, my eyes fail me because she is never commensurate with my representations of her. "The *interval* would never be *crossed.* Consummation would never take place, the idea itself being a delusion. One sex is not entirely consumable by the other. There is always a *remainder*" (Irigaray 1993, 14). This is the ethical moment because I must take into account this "remainder," this "inability to say what she represents."

Determining how to relate to this remainder, the unrepresented and unrepresentable, necessarily includes a determination of how I will care for myself. The decision will reflect, however inexactly, who I perceive myself to be and the nature of our relationship with each other and with the environment. Foucault identifies two options at this moment of decision: "to respond by intensifying all the recognizable marks of status or by seeking an adequate relationship with oneself"

(1986, 85). The intensification of status permits a *re*affirmation of self
and implies a pleasure at having arrived, once again, at an understanding of who one is. When status becomes preeminent, the fluctuating
intensities of an open relationship are rigidified by the definition of a
concrete ego-identity; the mobility of the other is checked when it is
decided that authority and privilege must be maintained. Seeking an
adequate relationship implies a disjunction between the existing image
of the self and the experience of the "other." There is a recognition that
within a relationship the vectors of force that articulate the distances
and differences between two subjects are constantly shifting and that
there is a need to be responsive to those variations. In this context the
self lacks solidity, and self-representations require a continual process
of reassessment and adjustment. Although this position lacks stability,
there is at least the possibility that a reciprocal and fluid interaction
with another can be developed. It is to this option that we must turn
our attention.

The Politics of Retreat

Acknowledging and accepting the necessity of keeping intersubjective
relations fluid is requisite to the open-ended process of developing "an
adequate relationship with oneself," because, in seeming contradiction,
defining the "self" puts limits on the way a *relationship with another* can
be conceived. The tendency in defining a relation with the self is to look
inward. But introspection as a means of understanding the structures
of subjectivity is immobilizing, because the movement inward tends
toward either a concretization of a hypothetical construct of the self, or
toward the recognition of intensities that indicate not a solidity but an
absence. In either case subjectivity is conceptualized by refusing to
acknowledge the agency of others. She ceases to have dimension,
movement; she is denied *her* "remainder." Seeking the outlines of the
self makes it difficult to imagine interactions that encourage her to
experience herself. Reciprocity is truncated by the desire to define con-
clusively the differences that allow for the ecstatic recognition of the
self. The alternative to looking inward is to open outward, not in an
effort to reinscribe status but as a means of opening spaces in which
others are free to move, to experience themselves, to have a voice in
defining our relationship to each other.

Hans Magnus Enzensberger, speaking about the collapse of Eastern Europe, perceives in retreat a new kind of heroic act, "representing not victory, conquest and triumph, but renunciation, reduction and dismantling" (1990, 136). It is heroic because instead of claiming territory it is a dismantling of walls and allowing those who have been excluded greater latitude for movement. Such an act is, inevitably, a point of resistance, the moment in which relationships become relations of power. However, the experience of resistance must be juxtaposed to the effects of differentiation if an ethical response is to be determined. "We are never trapped by power: we can always modify its grip in determinate conditions and according to a precise strategy" (Foucault 1989c, 153). "The *non plus ultra* in the art of the possible consists of withdrawing from an untenable position" (Enzensberger 1990, 136). At the intersection of Foucault and Enzensberger lies the basis of what the latter calls "the politics of retreat" (1990, 142), of what the former perceives as an aesthetics of existence. Cultivating the self as an ethical being necessitates an evaluation of the relative positions of the self and the other, not as if on an imaginary level field but cognizant of the hierarchies of status, of authority and privilege; not only in terms of the momentary context, but the historically and socially determined boundaries of difference. This cannot be an abstract exercise or one that is merely a practice of self-reflection. It needs to be grounded in the material resistance of the moment; and in the perception of that moment the "other" must be understood not only through our representations of her, but with consideration for "her inability to say what she represents"—the remainder of her subjectivity. And in that moment, to recognize through empathy our own unrepresentability, not as a sign of existential difference but of similitude.

This is the moment of reciprocity: when others can explore for themselves ways of experiencing their remainder—not just for us, but for themselves. But retreating is not easy. The positions we occupy are not selected casually, but reflect the complex interaction of the force of demand, experience, ideology, and the administrations of culture. To step back is to put into question the habitual practices that define our subjectivity. "Retreating from a position you have held involves not only surrendering the middle ground, but also giving up a part of yourself" (Enzensberger 1990, 137). This is the second point of resistance. There is an external moment when, in our interactions with others, we are forced to confront the contradictions between who we perceive ourselves to be and the ground on which we position ourselves as subjects, the relationship between self-image and the pleasures of the body. We stand on both sides of Heiner Müller's bulletproof glass: knowing the change that is needed is against ourselves.

But caring for the self is not altruistic. To paraphrase Michel Foucault, the cultivation of the self is "a political ordering of life, not through an enslavement of [the self], but through an affirmation of the self." The opening of spaces will never be accomplished through self-repression. Actively resisting the force of demand as it flows through the channels of subjectivity will not result in change but in the reactionary and violent desire to conserve—to return, in new forms and under the guise of new rationalities, to the same. The backlash confronted by virtually every demand for change, whether by the Right or the Left, stands as proof. For change to be effected, new pleasures, new modes of expression must be defined, based not on the self, but on the recognition that caring for the self is caring for the other.

The potential for change lies in reciprocity, in the recognition that the objectification, the negation of the other is ultimately impoverishing to the one who objectifies because the only possible return is that of the same—the infinite regress of a reflected self-image. But in a reciprocal relationship the experience of witnessing the other experiencing herself for herself can be incredibly enriching. To know that by retreating from a position of status it is possible to empower another is, in itself, empowering. To retreat, say in the context of sexual relations, is not to pull back into the self, to deny difference, but to embrace difference, to

> take seriously at last the "hetero" in heterosexuality, which means the heterogeneity in us, on us, through us, and also take seriously the "sexuality," which means, I think, giving up, precisely, heterosexuality, that oppressive representation of the sexual as act, complementarity, two sexes, coupling. (Heath 1987a, 22)

To retreat is to step back from indefensible binaries whether of sexuality, race, class, or ethnicity, categories that construct differences in order to preserve particular pleasures. It is to be attendant to the voice(s) of the remainder, the glyphs of intensity, the unrepresentable.

There is a danger here, as at every step, and that is the desire to look, to seek in the "other" that which cannot be articulated in language. To return to the discourse of the eye is to name her, once again, mystery, the dark and unknown. To look is to limit space because every articulation she expresses is met with the gaze, with seeking either the revelation of the new, which places the monstrous burden of novelty on her, or the outlines of the self in the folds of the "other," which reinstates her objectification. Nothing is changed.

In Habermas's reading of George Herbert Mead's theory of subjectivity, change is not a question of devising new practices, but of coming to terms with the processes by which identity is derived. "Accordingly, an identity that always remains mine, namely, my self-understanding as an autonomously acting and individuated being, can stabilize itself only if I find recognition as a person, and as this person" (Habermas 1992, 192). Identity as an individual is defined through intersubjective experiences, through mutual recognition, not autonomous actions. An aesthetics of subjectivity, in the sense of Foucault, requires a willingness to perceive others as subjects.

> The independent performances that are here demanded from the subjects consist of something *different* than rational choices steered by one's own preferences; what these subjects must perform is the kind of moral and existential self-reflection that is not possible without the one taking up the perspective of the other. Only thus can there emerge a new kind of social integration among individuals who are individualized and not merely manipulated. The participants must themselves generate their socially integrated forms of life by recognizing each other as autonomous subjects capable of action and, beyond this, as individuated beings who vouch for the continuity of the life histories for which they have taken responsibility. (Habermas 1992, 199)

Reciprocity is the willingness to acknowledge others by "taking up the perspective of the other," "by recognizing each other as autonomous subjects capable of action" and not mere surfaces in which we can see ourselves reflected. Recognizing others also means allowing them to take responsibility for their "life histories." To do this means resisting evaluating lives and lifestyles prior to intersubjective encounters, or at least recognizing when we do it. Such prejudices erect boundaries that resist recognition and encourage manipulation rather than reciprocal interaction.

To hear before interpretation, on the other hand, is to accept what she is willing to give; is to be attendant to how she expresses herself. To hear is to step back from assumptions of authority, to open a space in which she can exist for herself, can give what she chooses to give. To hear is to initiate the possibility of reciprocity.

> Life always open to what happens. To the fleeting touch of what has not yet found a setting. To the grace of a future that none can control. That will or will not happen. But while one waits for it, any possession of the world or of the other is suspended. A future coming not measured by the transcendence of death but by the call to birth of the self and the other. For which each one arranges and rearranges the environment, the body . . . without closing off any aspect of a room, a house, an identity. (Irigaray 1993, 186)

In Irigaray's vision of love within sexual difference there is the recognition of silence, of waiting without assumptions of possession, as a value rather than an opportunity. And in that recognition is the possibility of experiencing her intensities.

Caring for the self as caring for the other carries no guarantees: "any new ethical system will presumably bring new dangers" (Dreyfus and Rabinow 1983, 263). One problem that can be foreseen is the issue of reciprocity. The barriers against trust are well fortified; and to acknowledge similitude, to accept contradiction within oneself, and to open oneself to hearing without interpretation necessitates becoming vulnerable—it is implicit in a politics of retreat. There always exists the possibility that the processes of intersubjectivity will breakdown. On what ground do we differentiate between self-expression and appropriation? With what criteria can we decide whether or not the pleasures we are receiving from the relationship are mutual? Jessica Benjamin, exploring issues of domination and intersubjectivity in *The Bonds of Love*, acknowledges the inevitability of conflict but understands it can be an opportunity rather than a finality.

> If the denial of recognition does not become frozen into unmovable relationships, the play of power need not be hardened into domination. As the practice of psychoanalysis reveals, breakdown and renewal are constant possibilities: the crucial issue is finding the point at which breakdown occurs and the point at which it is pos-

sible to recreate tension and restore the condition of recognition. (Benjamin 1988, 223)

Such a determination requires a continual process of defining the qualitative differences between pleasures, separating the joys of sharing from the solipsism of self-reflection. "There are only reciprocal relations, and the perpetual gaps between intentions in relation to one another" (Foucault 1989d, 267). Reciprocity implies a sharing of responsibilities and the exchange of pleasures. Caring for the self as caring for the other, hearing rather than binding other voices, defining alternative topographies for experiencing the self, taking pleasure in the pleasures of the other is to begin to answer the question with which this chapter began: "Are we able to have an ethics of acts and their pleasures which would be able to take into account the pleasure of the other."

Works Cited

Abish, Walter. 1980. *How German Is It: Wie Deutsch Ist Es.* New York: New Directions Books.

Althusser, Louis. 1971. *Lenin and Philosophy and Other Essays.* Trans. Ben Brewster. New York: Monthly Review Press.

Artaud, Antonin. 1958. *The Theater and Its Double.* Trans. Mary Caroline Richards. New York: Grove Press.

———. 1965. "Correspondence with Jacques Riviere." Trans. Bernard Frechtman. *Artaud Anthology.* Ed. Jack Hirschman. San Francisco: City Lights Books.

Bank, Rosemarie. 1989. "Self as Other: Sam Shepard's *Fool for Love* and *A Lie of the Mind.*" *Feminist Rereadings of Modern American Drama.* Ed. June Schlueter. Rutherford, N.J.: Fairleigh Dickinson University Press.

Barber, Stephen. 1993. *Antonin Artaud: Blows and Bombs.* London: Faber and Faber.

Beckett, Samuel. 1984. *The Collected Short Plays.* New York: Grove Press.

Begosian, Eric. 1988. *Talk Radio.* New York: Vintage Books.

Benjamin, Jessica. 1988. *Bonds of Love: Psychoanalysis, Feminism, and the Problem of Domination.* New York: Pantheon Books.

Benjamin, Walter. 1969. *Illuminations.* Trans. Harry Zohn. Ed. Hannah Arendt. New York: Schocken Books.

Blau, Herbert. 1982a. *Blooded Thought: Occasions of Theatre.* New York: Performing Arts Publications.

———. 1982b. *Take Up the Bodies: Theater at the Vanishing Point.* Urbana: University of Illinois Press.

———. 1987. *The Eye of Prey: Subversions of the Postmodern.* Bloomington: Indiana University Press.

———. 1992. *To All Appearances: Ideology and Performance.* New York: Routledge.

Bly, Robert. 1990. *Iron John: A Book about Men.* Reading, Mass.: Addison-Wesley.

Braidotti, Rosi. 1987. "Envy; or, With My Brains and Your Looks." *Men in Feminism.* Ed. Alice Jardine and Paul Smith. New York: Methuen.

Brod, Harry. 1990. "Scholarly Studies of Men: The New Field Is an Essential Complement to Women's Studies." *Chronicle of Higher Education,* 21 March, B2–3.

Butler, Judith. 1993. *Bodies That Matter: On the Discursive Limits of "Sex."* New York: Routledge.

———. 1990. *Gender Trouble: Feminism and the Subversion of Identity.* New York: Routledge.

Case, Sue-Ellen. 1995a. "Performing Lesbian in the Space of Technology: Part I." *Theatre Journal* 47 (March): 1–18.

———. 1995b. "Performing Lesbian in the Space of Technology: Part II." *Theatre Journal* 47 (October): 329–43.

Deleuze, Gilles, and Félix Guattari. 1983. *Anti-Oedipus: Capitalism and Schizophrenia.* Trans. Robert Hurley, Mark Seem, and Helen R. Lane. Minneapolis: University of Minnesota Press.

———. 1987. *A Thousand Plateaus.* Trans. Brian Massumi. Minneapolis: University of Minnesota Press.

Derrida, Jacques. 1978. *Writing and Difference.* Trans. Alan Bass. Chicago: University of Chicago Press.

———. 1987. "Women in the Beehive: A Seminar with Jacques Derrida." Trans. James Adner. *Men in Feminism.* Ed. Alice Jardine and Paul Smith. New York: Methuen.

Dreyfus, Hubert L., and Paul Rabinow. 1983. *Michel Foucault: Beyond Structuralism and Hermeneutics.* 2d ed. Chicago: University of Chicago Press.

Duras, Marguerite. 1981. "Smothered Creativity." *New French Feminisms.* Ed. Elaine Marks and Isabelle de Courtivron. New York: Schocken Books.

Elam, Keir. 1980. *The Semiotics of Theatre and Drama.* London: Methuen.

Enzensberger, Hans Magnus. 1990. "The State of Europe." Trans. Piers Spence. *Granta,* winter, 136–42.

Foucault, Michel. 1973. *The Order of Things.* New York: Vintage Books.

———. 1977. *Language, Counter-Memory, Practice,* ed. Donald F. Bouchard. Ithaca: Cornell University Press.

———. 1980. *The History of Sexuality,* vol. 1: *An Introduction.* Trans. Robert Hurley. New York: Vintage Books.

———. 1983. "On the Genealogy of Ethics: An Overview of Work in Progress." In *Michel Foucault: Beyond Structuralism and Hermeneutics,* by Hubert L. Dreyfus and Paul Rabinow. 2d ed. Chicago: University of Chicago Press.

———. 1986. *The History of Sexuality,* vol. 3: *The Care of the Self.* Trans. Robert Hurley. New York: Vintage Books.

———. 1989a. "An Aesthetics of Existence." Trans. John Johnston. *Foucault Live.* Ed. Sylvere Lotringer. New York: Semiotext(e).

———. 1989b. "The Concern for Truth." Trans. John Johnston. *Foucault Live.* Ed. Sylvere Lotringer. New York: Semiotext(e).

———. 1989c. "The End of the Monarchy of Sex." Trans. Dudley M. Marchi. *Foucault Live.* Ed. Sylvere Lotringer. New York: Semiotext(e).

———. 1989d. "An Ethics of Pleasure." Trans. Stephen Riggins. *Foucault Live.* Ed. Sylvere Lotringer. New York: Semiotext(e).

———. 1989e. "The Return of Morality." Trans. John Johnston. *Foucault Live.* Ed. Sylvere Lotringer. New York: Semiotext(e).

Freud, Sigmund. 1953–74. *The Standard Edition of the Complete Psychological Works of Sigmund Freud.* Ed. and trans. James Strachey. 21 vols. London: Hogarth.

Genet, Jean. 1966. *The Balcony.* Trans. Bernard Frechtman. New York: Grove Press.

Grant, Gary. 1993. "Shifting the Paradigm: Shepard, Myth, and the Transformation of Consciousness." *Modern Drama* 36 (March): 120–30.

Grosz, Elizabeth. 1994. *Volatile Bodies: Toward a Corporeal Feminism.* Bloomington: Indiana University Press.

Habermas, Jürgen. 1992. *Postmetaphysical Thinking: Philosophical Essays.* Trans. William Mark Hohengarten. Cambridge, Mass.: MIT Press.

Haedicke, Janet V. 1993. "'A Population [and Theater] at Risk': Battered Women in Henley's *Crimes of the Heart* and Shepard's *A Lie of the Mind.*" *Modern Drama* 36 (March): 83–95.

Hart, Lynda. 1989. "Sam Shepard's Spectacle of Impossible Heterosexuality: *Fool for Love.*" *Feminist Rereadings of Modern American Drama.* Ed. June Schlueter. Rutherford, N.J.: Fairleigh Dickinson University Press.

Hayles, N. Katherine. 1994. "Embodied Virtuality; or, How to Put Bodies Back into the Picture." Paper read at the Humanities Institute at SUNY Stony Brook.

Heath, Stephen. 1987a. "Male Feminism." *Men in Feminism.* Ed. Alice Jardine and Paul Smith. New York: Methuen.

———. 1987b. "Men in Feminism: Men and Feminist Theory." *Men in Feminism.* Ed. Alice Jardine and Paul Smith. New York: Methuen.

Irigaray, Luce. 1985. *Speculum of the Other Woman.* Trans. Gillian C. Gill. Ithaca: Cornell University Press.

———. 1993. *An Ethics of Sexual Difference.* Trans. Carolyn Burke and Gillian C. Gill. Ithaca: Cornell University Press.

Jardine, Alice. 1987. "Men in Feminism: Odor di Uomo or Compagnons de Route?" *Men in Feminism.* Ed. Alice Jardine and Paul Smith. New York: Methuen.

Jardine, Alice, and Paul Smith, eds. 1987. *Men in Feminism.* New York: Methuen.

Kamuf, Peggy. 1987. "Femmeninism." *Men in Feminism.* Ed. Alice Jardine and Paul Smith. New York: Methuen.

Kimmel, Michael. 1993. "Dudes and Don'ts: The Reclamation of Manhood in Contemporary Film." *Changing Men* 26 (summer–fall): 50–51.

Kroker, Arthur, and David Cook. 1988. *Postmodern Scene: Excremental Culture and Hyper-Aesthetics.* New York: St. Martin's Press.

Lacan, Jacques. 1977. *Ecrits: A Selection.* Trans. Alan Sheridan. New York: W. W. Norton.

Mayne, Judith. 1987. "Walking the *Tightrope* of Feminism and Male Desire." *Men in Feminism.* Ed. Alice Jardine and Paul Smith. New York: Methuen.

Müller, Heiner. 1984. *Hamletmachine and Other Texts for the Stage.* Trans. Carl Weber. New York: PAJ Publications.

———. 1989. *Explosion of a Memory.* Ed. and trans. Carl Weber. New York: PAJ Publications.

Phelan, Peggy. 1993. *Unmarked: The Politics of Performance.* London: Routledge.

———. 1995. "Thirteen Ways of Looking at *Choreographing Writing.*" *Choreographing History.* Ed. Susan Leigh Foster. Bloomington: Indiana University Press.

Roach, Joseph. 1995. "Bodies of Doctrine: Headshots, Jane Austen, and the Black Indians of Mardi Gras." *Choreographing History.* Ed. Susan Leigh Foster. Bloomington: Indiana University Press.

Rosen, Carol. 1993. "'Emotional Territory': An Interview with Sam Shepard." *Modern Drama* 36 (March): 1–11.

Ross, Andrew. 1987a. "Demonstrating Sexual Difference." *Men in Feminism.* Ed. Alice Jardine and Paul Smith. New York: Methuen.

———. 1987b. "No Question of Silence." *Men in Feminism.* Ed. Alice Jardine and Paul Smith. New York: Methuen.

Schvey, Henry I. 1993. "A Worm in the Wood: The Father-Son Relationship in the Plays of Sam Shepard." *Modern Drama* 36 (March). 12–26.

Shepard, Sam. 1977. "Visualization, Language, and the Inner Library." *Drama Review* T76 (December): 49–58.

———. 1981. *Sam Shepard: Seven Plays.* New York: Bantam Books.

———. 1986. *A Lie of the Mind; The War in Heaven: Angel's Monologue.* New York: New American Library.

Showalter, Elaine. 1987. "Critical Cross-Dressing: Male Feminists and the Woman of the Year." *Men in Feminism.* Ed. Alice Jardine and Paul Smith. New York: Methuen.

Smith, Joseph H., ed. 1991. *The World of Samuel Beckett.* Baltimore: Johns Hopkins University Press.

Smith, Paul. 1987. "Men in Feminism: Men and Feminist Theory." *Men in Feminism.* Ed. Alice Jardine and Paul Smith. New York: Methuen.

Strange, Douglas C. 1990. Letter to the editor. *Chronicle of Higher Education,* 11 April, B3.

Theweleit, Klaus. 1987. *Male Fantasies,* vol. 1: *Women, Floods, Bodies, History.* Trans. Stephen Conway. Minneapolis: University of Minnesota Press.

Thorne-Finch, Ron. 1992. *Ending the Silence: The Origins and Treatment of Male Violence against Women.* Toronto: University of Toronto Press.

Turner, Victor. 1982. *From Ritual to Theatre: The Human Seriousness of Play.* New York: PAJ Publications.

———. 1988. *The Anthropology of Performance.* New York: PAJ Publications.

Wheeler, Helen Rippier. 1990. Letter to the editor. *Chronicle of Higher Education,* 11 April, B3.

Index